Praise for Faith Deployed . . . Again

"*Faith Deployed . . . Again* emanates from the heart of Christ and flows through military wives who have experienced the ordeals that all hold in common. You will find a hug from Jesus on every page that will give light to an otherwise shadowy day, or the strength and courage necessary to persevere when weakness threatens your soul. What you will then discover within these pages is that the grace of the Lord Jesus Christ is truly sufficient for your every need! Moreover you will find that you will have become a river of healing to those around you—transformed from encouraged to encourager."

—BOB FLYNN, president/CEO,
Christian Military Fellowship

"Jocelyn Green again hits the ball out of the ballpark with *Faith Deployed . . . Again*, bringing hope, healing, and a feeling of connectedness with women everywhere who are touched by the life and service of a military member."

—REV. RAHNELLA ADSIT
Military Ministry of Campus Crusade for Christ, Intl.
Coauthor of *When War Comes Home—*
Christ-Centered Healing for Wives of Combat Veterans
President of Branches of Valor Inc.
and executive-director of Sisters of Valor Retreats

"*Faith Deployed . . . Again* is a masterpiece for military wives—a life-application manual loaded with wisdom from God's Word as told by women intimately familiar with the daily challenges of life in today's military. Inspiring, encouraging, faith-building, hope-giving—this book is all that and more!"

—CHAPLAIN COL. SCOTT MCCHRYSTAL (USA Ret),
Mil/VA rep and endorser,
Assemblies of God Chaplaincy Ministries

"Daily reminders of the truth we find in God's Word are so important for a military spouse. In her new book, *Faith Deployed . . . Again*, Jocelyn Green creates yet another wonderful opportunity for military spouses to focus on God's truth while relating to the shared experiences of other spouses. Since I know many of these contributors personally, reading this book is like listening to friends over coffee and being reminded of the blessings God gives us even in the midst of the challenging season of deployment."

—SARA HORN, founder of Wives of Faith (wivesoffaith.org) and author of *GOD Strong: A Military Wife's Spiritual Survival Guide* and *Tour of Duty: Preparing Our Hearts for Deployment*

"The deployed one isn't the only spouse facing battles. *Faith Deployed . . . Again* provides real, honest, and transparent snapshots from spouses from every service and stage of deployment and life. Do you feel afraid, alone, abandoned, lost, depressed? You'll find tremendous encouragement within these pages. Marrying 'into the military' and sacrificing during my deployment, my wife would have been greatly blessed through these powerful stories, inspiring quotations, and transformational truths. God is working in deep ways within our Armed Forces and families in the midst of the challenges of deployment. May this book take you deeper in Him, as it has for me."

—DAVE MEAD
Director of Navigator Military Ministry
Colonel in the Army Reserve

"Everyone needs a friend, and especially those who wait at home while their loved one deploys and so often to a dangerous and lonely place somewhere on the globe. Offering such a friend in *Faith Deployed . . . Again* is author Jocelyn Green in her second work on this crucially important subject. This wonderful collection of timely meditations comes from fellow wives who have already been there on the spiritual battlefield of the home front and tasted the daily victories that only God can provide. Thank God for this timely book that fills a critical need in the lives of military families, and for Jocelyn Green and her fellow spiritual warriors faithfully engaged in support of those families and their deployed spouses."

—CDR. VICTOR PRIMEAUX (USCG Ret)
Director of Ministries to Coast Guard Forces and Families, Christian Military Fellowship (CMF)

"Again, Jocelyn compiles the right mix of stories of military wives standing on the promises of God. This book brings godly help, encouraging stories, and new battle buddies into military wives' lives for each battle both during and between deployments. We can't do it alone. In fact, we are not doing it alone, and I'm so glad this book is a reminder of that: God's presence is with us."

—STARLETT HENDERSON, coauthor of *1001 Things to Love About Military Life* and cofounder of Army Wife Network

"Jocelyn Green has her finger on the pulse of military wives. She has been one, and she listens and connects to their heartfelt stories. Jocelyn knows how to communicate a hope-filled message to these warriors on the home front! The more we serve these heroic families, the more we realize the sacrifices they make on our behalf to protect our freedom. Read this book; buy additional copies and resource every military wife you can get it to. They will be blessed by your desire to speak life into their great hearts."

—DR. GARY and BARB ROSBERG
Authors of *6 Secrets to a Lasting Love*, Pre-Deployment Military Marriage DVD, *Dilemmas and Breakthroughs*

"Hope and encouragement—I can think of no greater gift to give the military home front. *Faith Deployed . . . Again* is Christian military wives and mothers cheering, encouraging, challenging, guiding, mentoring us in our journey to know the Author of Hope, Jesus Christ, while we combat the challenges of the military lifestyle."

—BENITA KOEMAN, founder of
OperationWeAreHere.com

Faith DEPLOYED ...Again

More Daily Encouragement

for Military Wives

JOCELYN GREEN

MOODY PUBLISHERS

CHICAGO

Published in association with the literary agency of Credo Communications in Grand Rapids, Michigan, www.credocommunications.net.

Edited by Pam Pugh
Interior design: Smartt Guys design
Author Photo: Paul Kestel
Cover design: DogEared Design
Cover image: SuperStock 1779R-3993 (RF)

Library of Congress Cataloging-in-Publication Data

Green, Jocelyn.
Faith deployed—again : more daily encouragement for military wives / Jocelyn Green.
p. cm.
ISBN 978-0-8024-5251-1
1. Military spouses—Prayers and devotions. 2. Wives—Prayers and devotions. I. Title.
BV4528.15.G72 2011
242'.6435—dc22
2011009047

Also available as an EBook 978-0-8024-7832-0

Moody Publishers is committed to caring wisely for God's creation and uses recycled paper whenever possible. The paper in this book consists of 10 percent post-consumer waste.

We hope you enjoy this book from Moody Publishers. Our goal is to provide high-quality, thought-provoking books and products that connect truth to your real needs and challenges. For more information on other books and products written and produced from a biblical perspective, go to www.moodypublishers.com or write to:

Moody Publishers
820 N. LaSalle Boulevard
Chicago, IL 60610

1 3 5 7 9 10 8 6 4 2

Printed in the United States of America

Dedication

To the wives of all those who serve our country through the US armed forces, especially those whose lives have been drastically altered since the terrorist attacks on September 11, 2001.

You hear, O Lord, the desire of the afflicted;
You encourage them, and you listen to their cry,
Defending the fatherless and the oppressed,
in order that man, who is of the earth, may terrify no more.
PSALM 10:17–18

Contents

Introduction 15

Section One

Basic Training: Guiding Principles for Military Living

Vision Check 18
Faith That Moves Mountains 20
The Reluctant Military Wife 22
Complaining vs. Confession 24
Trail Markers 26
Soul Talk 28
An Outcry 30
Treasures of Darkness 32
Loving the Difficult Ones 34
Rethinking My Rituals 36
Whatever! 38
Vengeance Is the Lord's 40
The Work of Perseverance 42
Harvesting the Soul 44

Section Two

Intimate Allies: Protecting Your Military Marriage

Committed 48
Predeployment Distance 50
Perfection in Marriage 52
To Love Like Christ 54
The Submariner Treatment 56
The Powerful Act of Submission 58
Communicating Expectations 60
"He Owes Me" 62
Loving without Seeing 64

Holiness before Happiness 66
More Than a Constant Dripping 68
The Path to Infidelity 70
Not the Man I Married 72
Two Are Better Than One 74

Section Three
Tour of Duty: Overcoming Deployments and Other Separations
More Than Surviving 78
Finding Joy 80
Broken and Alone 82
Buying Coffee 84
The God Who Sees Me 86
Bridging the Parenting Gap 88
Unexpected 90
Little Indiscretions 92
The Absent Leader 94
Change Is Good 96
Watches of the Night 98
Gimmes for Teens 100
Daddy's Presence 102
Never-ending Days, Everlasting God 104
Held Up 106

Section Four
Soul Armor: Guarding against Spiritual Attacks
The Armor of Light 110
Enemy Tactics 112
Do Not Fear 114
Voices 116
Nightmares 118
Freedom from Suspicion 120
The Roaring Lion 122
Anticipatory Grief 124

Filling the Void.....126
When Fear Attacks.....128
The Pursuit of Peace.....130
Roll the Stone Away!.....132
Surrender.....134
Out of the Darkness.....136

Section Five
Stationed in Christ: Dwelling in the Lord, Near and Far
The Places We Go.....140
To Be Rooted.....142
Traveling Light.....144
Placing Our Identity in Christ.....146
Trusting God Overseas.....148
The Daily Office.....150
The Exact Time and Place.....152
Remember Me.....154
Soulmaking.....156
Moving . . . with Children.....158
Bloom Where You're Planted.....160
In the Cave.....162
Devotions or Devotion?.....164
Safe House.....166

Section Six
In God's Service: Living for the Lord
The Choice We Have.....170
Finding Your Ministry.....172
Soul Food.....174
An Ordinary Military Wife.....176
Discipling Others.....178
Unforgotten.....180
Scars.....182
A Quiet Place.....184
Prayer Warrior.....186

Honor Your Mother by Marriage 188
A Hospitable Home 190
My Plan or Yours, Lord? 192
The Ministry of Compassion 194
Worn Out and Weary 196

Section Seven

Home Front Hope: Moving Forward in God's Strength

Posted by Families 200
Turtle Shells 202
What God Has Promised 204
Infertility's Silent Sorrow 206
Hidden Rainbows 208
Your Financial Future 210
Seeing in the Dark 212
One Day at a Time 214
Caring for the Wounded Warrior 216
Overcoming Labels 218
Waiting on the Lord 220
When Morale is Low 222
Declaring War on Debt 224
Unresolved 226
Band of Sisters 228

Section Eight

For Blue Star Moms: Trusting God with Your Service Member

Letting Go 232
Warrior Angels 234
Solitude 236
Secret Fears 238
Wait Training 240
The Formula 242
God, My Soldier's Parent 244
A New Normal 246
Accepting Grace . . . Again 248

We Are at War 250
Knowing Jesus Personally 252
Stay Encouraged 254

Notes 255
Acknowledgments 259
Meet the Contributors 260
About the Author 270

Introduction

Dear Military Wife,

I salute you. Military life is never easy, but the last decade of frequent and extended deployments has placed enormous strain on you as you have supported your family. It's time, for a change, for you to be the one getting support. And I can think of no better source of encouragement than our Sovereign God, and His Word.

Whether your military family experiences deployments or not, military life requires that we all deploy our faith in order to respond biblically to each trial we face. *Faith Deployed . . . Again* was written by nearly thirty Christian women from every branch of service to show you how the Bible applies to what you experience as a military wife. While our soldiers fight physical enemies, those on the home front battle what is unseen: discouragement, loneliness, fear, and more.

Because so many military wives are finding themselves as mothers of service members now, as well, there are bonus devotions at the end of the book written by and for Blue Star moms.

Faith Deployed . . . Again will encourage you in many ways, but more than anything, I hope it encourages you to seek out what God has to say to you through the Bible in your own quiet time with Him. He is a personal God, and He has something to say to you. I pray that you know Him personally already. If you don't, or if you're unsure, please see the appendix "Knowing Jesus Personally" on this subject in the back of the book.

My prayer for each of you is that after reading this book, you'll be able to say to yourself, like Deborah did, "March on, my soul; be strong!" (Judges 5:21).

Blessings,

Jocelyn Green

Section One

BASIC TRAINING:

Guiding Principles for Military Living

For physical training is of some value, but godliness has value for all things, holding promise for both the present life and the life to come.

1 TIMOTHY 4:8

by Jocelyn Green

Vision CHECK

Taste and see that the Lord is good;
blessed is the one who takes refuge in him.
PSALM 34:8

WHEN ROB AND I MARRIED, we chose the hymn "Be Thou My Vision" to be played while we lit our unity candle. I had always loved the lyrics, but I had no idea how perfect they would prove to be not just for a single moment during a wedding ceremony, but for the day-to-day military lifestyle I was entering into.

So much of how we think, feel, and live depends on our vision—what we choose to see in any given situation. In fact, I believe that the difference between being simply concerned or being consumed by worry rides on where we tend to focus our sight.

In her book *Having a Mary Heart in a Martha World*, Joanna Weaver says, "Pastor and teacher Gary E. Gilley sums up the difference like this: 'Worry is allowing problems and distress to come between us and the heart of God. It is the view that God has somehow lost control of the situation and we cannot trust Him. A legitimate concern presses us closer to the heart of God and causes us to lean and trust on Him all the more.' *Concern draws us to God. Worry pulls us from Him.*"[1]

Military wives (indeed, everyone on the planet!) will always have something to be concerned about. There are issues that simply cannot be ignored. But if we have done everything we can to help solve the problem and still find ourselves obsessing over it, we've crossed that line from concern to worry and find ourselves in dangerous territory.

The key to banishing worry from your heart is surprisingly simple. I look at it this way: Your heart (and mine) has a limited capacity. The best way to get rid of the negative thoughts is to crowd them out with something else bigger and more beautiful: worship of the One who holds everything in His powerful and capable hands. In other words, stop focusing on the root of your worries and shift your gaze to the Lord. It won't make the troubles disappear, but it sure will help you to stop staring at them all day long!

King David was a master at this. Psalm 10 begins with "Why, O Lord, do you stand far off? Why do you hide yourself in times of trouble?" But by the time he gets to the end of the chapter, he changes his tune to: "You hear, O Lord, the desire of the afflicted; you encourage them, and you listen to their cry, defending the fatherless and the oppressed, in order that man, who is of the earth, may terrify no more" (verses 17–18). Did you see that? He turned his worry into worship.

The next time your heart is troubled, check your vision. Focus on God and on His unchanging character. Trust in who He is and the promises He provides in Scripture, rather than what is going on around you.

Ask

What am I most worried about today?
What can I praise God for instead?

Pray

Lord, please forgive my tendency to worry about things I can't control. Help me draw closer to You and replace my anxiety by meditating on Your Word. In Jesus' Name, Amen.

by Tonya Nash

Faith THAT MOVES MOUNTAINS

"Have faith in God," Jesus answered. "I tell you the truth, if anyone says to this mountain, 'Go, throw yourself into the sea,' and does not doubt in his heart but believes that what he says will happen, it will be done for him. Therefore I tell you, whatever you ask for in prayer, believe that you have received it, and it will be yours."

MARK 11:22–24

★ ★ ★

NOTHING SPOILS THE JOY of an engagement like hearing that your fiancé is deploying to war, with no guarantees of returning in time for the wedding. But that's what happened to me.

Jamie and I got engaged November 10, 2002. We prayed about our wedding date and both felt that June 7, 2003 was perfect. Three weeks after our engagement, Jamie received orders to deploy in support of Operation Iraqi Freedom. I was devastated! I asked Jamie if we should postpone the wedding, but he was adamant about not changing our wedding date. We continued to plan our wedding while he was deployed through e-mail, letters, and phone calls.

Opposition often presented itself, but Jamie and I prayed to God and believed by faith that he would get home in time for the wedding. On April 30, a miracle happened. The command allowed a few people to go home who had important, life-changing events coming up. Jamie arrived home on May 3, a little over a month before our wedding, just in time for the groomsmen's fitting party.

I'll admit that at times our faith became weak, especially during that month of April. But the Bible says we only need faith the size of a mustard seed to accomplish the impossible (Matthew 17:20).

Abraham believed by faith when God told him that his descendants would outnumber the stars in the sky, despite the fact that he was well beyond the age of childbearing. Because of his faith, God credited it to him as righteousness (Genesis 15:1–6).

Mary believed when the angel Gabriel told her she would give birth, while still a virgin. Joseph could have broken off the engagement. But Mary continued to believe by faith and maintained a positive outlook saying, "I am the Lord's servant. May it be to me as you have said" (Luke 1:38).

Are you struggling in an area of faith? Connect with positive people who will stand in faith with you and lift you up in prayer. Study the Word of God and put your faith in action, for the Bible declares, "Faith without deeds is dead" (James 2:26).

Ask

Am I exercising my faith?
Do I believe God for the seemingly impossible?

Prayer

Dear Lord, strengthen me when my faith gets weak. Help me to have childlike faith in the midst of challenging circumstances. In Jesus' Name, Amen.

by Pattie Reitz

THE *Reluctant* MILITARY WIFE

Have I not commanded you? Be strong and courageous. Do not be terrified; do not be discouraged, for the Lord your God will be with you wherever you go.

JOSHUA 1:9

NO.

That's what I said when my husband said he wanted to go into full-time active duty military ministry.

I am not one of those women who willingly married a man in uniform. I'd married a preacher passionate about sharing God's Word with His people and winning souls to Christ. When he joined the reserves in the wake of 9/11, I barely batted an eye. The camouflage in the closet was new, and he was gone a little more, but in most ways our life was the same. That is, until he decided to leave the pastorate and join the military full-time.

I said no, but God would not release His calling on my husband's life. I wrestled with God, and I would not budge. "This is not what I signed up for, Lord!" I cried. "This was not in the plan!"

Throughout the long weeks in which my husband filled out paperwork and waited to hear if there was a place for him, I cried and threw a fit in my heart. I argued with God, stomped my feet, and was pretty upset with Him.

But then God reminded me of what he had said to His people through Joshua in Joshua 1:9 (quoted above).

There it was: *For the Lord your God is with you wherever you go.* This verse suddenly applied to me in a very real way. I was not alone. In fact, in the first chapter, God tells Joshua *three* times not to be afraid. Remember Joshua is the man who led the unorthodox charge to conquer the walled city of Jericho (Joshua 6)! If such a courageous man needed reassurance, we are certainly allowed to need it as well. Jeremiah 17:7 also reassures us: "Blessed is the man who trusts in the Lord, whose confidence is in him."

Whether your marriage began with the military already woven into its fabric, or you came into the military life later on as I did, chances are you know what it's like to be reluctant over something that was not part of "the plan"—a PCS, another TDY, a deployment. Rest in the knowledge that even if your life is not going according to your plan and you're feeling reluctant to follow God's call, you are not alone. God's promises are steadfast and true, and "do not fear" is just as relevant today for you as it was for Joshua.

As Deuteronomy 31:8 says, "The Lord himself goes before you and will be with you; he will never leave you nor forsake you. Do not be afraid; do not be discouraged."

In what ways are you supportive of your husband's calling into military service? How are you learning to depend on God's promises even when His plans don't line up with your own?

Pray

Lord, I claim Your promise that You are with me wherever I go. I rest in the assurance that You have led us into this military life, and You will continue to lead and guide us always. In Jesus' Name, Amen.

by Leeana Tankersley

COMPLAINING VS. *Confession*

Carry each other's burdens, and in this way you will fulfill the law of Christ.
GALATIANS 6:2

"WE KNEW WHAT we were getting into when we signed up for this marriage. We have no right to complain." Have you ever heard or said that line before?

Some of us have gotten good, maybe even too good, at coping. We steel ourselves into this pillar of strength, and we challenge anything to penetrate our armor. Meanwhile, we may or may not be feeling that same way on the inside, underneath our self-protective layers.

The problem is that we get used to living split off from our true selves. We become accustomed to denying what's actually going on inside us, and this creates a person who cannot be honest about her pain, cannot let others see her weakness, and cannot tolerate any kind of authentic struggle in others.

This woman sends the subtle (or not so subtle) message to her friends and to her children that the real winners are those who never let anyone see them sweat.

How incredibly isolating this behavior becomes for everyone. Yes, others may see us as amazingly stalwart, but they will never see us approachable. This keeps everyone dancing around each other at a safe distance, never really able to offer help and support.

So how do we decipher between complaining and true confession? Complaining is all about staying stuck, rehearsing the injustices with no desire to see things differently, change behavior, or receive support.

Confessing is something different altogether. Honest confession is an externalizing of an inward conversation for the purpose of gaining insight, releasing a burden, or admitting reality. Confession leads to movement and helps us get out of the grind of merely coping. It opens doors to growth and change because it is an act of congruence. By externalizing—sharing—our true state of affairs, we are better able to receive the help we really need.

It's risky to show need. Whether the need is emotional or financial or any other kind, being "needy" is kind of passé and, well, burdensome. I want to be the kind of person who flies through life with answers and resources and decorum and brilliant ease. I want to be a "have," not a "have not."

Still, I have a choice. I can cover up my need and miss an opportunity for true authenticity; or I can take a big risk and admit that I just might need some help and support. A friend once told me that when we share our burdens with others, the weight we are carrying is divided between those listening, and our load is immediately lightened—carrying and being carried.

Is my pride and sense of control keeping me from getting the support I really need? Am I willing to listen to others and lovingly carry their burdens as well?

God, I want to be strong, but I need safe places where I can be weak, too. Show me how to allow someone else to help carry my burdens. In Jesus' Name, Amen.

by Sarah Ball

Trail MARKERS

All Scripture is God-breathed and is useful for teaching, rebuking, correcting and training in righteousness, so that the servant of God may be thoroughly equipped for every good work.
2 TIMOTHY 3:16–17

★ ★ ★

"THERE HE IS! THERE'S DADDY!" my daughter yelled. It was an early spring morning, and my kids and I were standing alongside a wooded trail in Virginia. My husband jogged up the trail and past us toward the next checkpoint in the fifty-mile trail run.

Rather than following smooth roads or footpaths, trail runners scramble over logs, navigate puddles, and weave around boulders. More often than not, the trail is a barely visible line up a rocky slope. When the trail disappears, runners look for a splash of paint or a ribbon on a tree to indicate the path. A missed marker might mean a wrong turn and an extra mile or two of running in the wrong direction.

We are all engaged in a lifelong trail run. We'd like to follow smooth footpaths, but life keeps throwing boulders and logs in our way. We may hope that a relationship with Christ will lead us to an easier path, but God's Word does not promise carefree living.

In 2 Timothy 3, the apostle Paul writes to his young protégé Timothy, telling him what to expect from a life of following Christ. Paul reminds Timothy of the many persecutions that Paul endured during his ministry and warns Timothy that "all who desire to live godly in Christ Jesus will suffer persecution" (verse12). Paul reminds Timothy of the importance of Scripture—for instruction, for correction, for equipping the child of God for every good work.

When we are exhausted from running and surrounded by obstacles, we may wonder, "Am I on the right path? Did I take a wrong turn somewhere?" With boulders on every side, we begin to feel as if we have been left without a marker to guide us. Paul's challenge to Timothy becomes our challenge as well, to continue pressing forward in the way we have been taught, following the guidance of God's Word in everything.

God has given you His Word to provide your trail markers. Find a Bible reading plan that will keep you reading and learning Scripture daily. Your path may not become easy, but God's Word will thoroughly equip you to continue running in the direction God gives you.

Ask

How am I actively equipping myself with God's Word each day? How has God's Word provided guidance to my life recently?

Pray

Dear Father, thank You for the gift of Your Word and for its ability to instruct, teach, and equip me. As I encounter obstacles in my path today, please bring to mind the Scriptures I have learned to guide me. Help me to continue running in the way that You lead. In Jesus' Name, Amen.

by Jocelyn Green

Soul TALK

For as he thinks within himself, so he is.
PROVERBS 23:7 NASB

★ ★ ★

NINE O'CLOCK in the morning, and the sun still wasn't up in Homer, Alaska. Darkness rested heavily, like a shroud upon my house, and just as heavily on my heart.

"It's happening again," I told myself. Years earlier, I had been clinically depressed. And though God healed me, I still felt vulnerable to sinking back into that pit of despair. And by predicting it, I unwittingly created a self-fulfilling prophecy.

But when I trained myself to say, "It's just a bad day, just one bad day" instead, I no longer felt doomed to repeat the depression of my past. I felt like a normal military wife who has normal feelings, good days and bad days.

What we tell ourselves matters. Our self talk—whether silent or audible— directs both our attitudes and our actions. Proverbs 18:21 says, "The tongue has the power of life and death." Proverbs 23:7 (quoted above) tells us we are who we *think* we are. It is vital that what we say to ourselves matches up with the truths of Scripture.

In the book of Mark, we meet a woman who had been bleeding for twelve years. "When she heard about Jesus, she came up behind him in the crowd and touched his cloak, because she thought, 'If I just touch his clothes, I will be healed.' Immediately her bleeding stopped and she felt in her body that she was freed from her suffering" (Mark 5:27–29).

In her book *Self Talk, Soul Talk*, Jennifer Rothschild explains:

> The most important thing to note here isn't that she talked to herself. It's what she told herself that matters. . . . Counseling ourselves to act upon truth, coaching ourselves, and cheering ourselves on to make good choices—these are both healthy and wise. Wise soul talk pushes us over the edge to help us overcome our issues. In this story, the woman with the hemorrhage clearly benefited by telling herself that she would be healed if she touched Jesus' robe.[2]

We can follow this woman's example when our "soul talk"—words of truth that can heal us—directs us to wrench our gaze from our own problems to rest fully on Christ for a moment. My own self talk of "It's just a bad day" was a good start, but would have been better soul talk if I had added more Bible-based truth to it: "Why are you so downcast, O my soul? Why so disturbed within me? Put your hope in God, for I will yet praise him, my Savior and my God" (Psalm 43:5).

Try it for yourself. Instead of telling yourself what's wrong with your life, try "I have learned to be content whatever the circumstances" (Philippians 4:11). The next time you think, "I can't do it anymore," tell yourself "I can do everything through him who gives me strength" (Philippians 4:13).

Ask

What do I tell myself that causes more discouragement? Which truths from Scripture should I be telling myself instead?

Pray

Lord, help me notice what I tell myself throughout the day so I can identify how that helps or hurts me. Please help me train myself to base my soul talk on Scripture. In Jesus' Name, Amen.

by Leeana Tankersley

AN Outcry

But I cry to you for help, O Lord; in the morning my prayer comes before you. Why, O Lord, do you reject me and hide your face from me?
PSALM 88:13–14

I'VE HAD AN on-again-off-again relationship with prayer. At times, prayer has felt like the only lifeline I've had left. Other times, it has felt as ineffective as screaming into a tin can with a string tied to it.

I've had to give myself permission to wonder if prayer even makes a difference, to question whether or not my pleas actually turn the hand of God in any direction at all. Is God so cryptic and callous that He asks us to pray but then doesn't actually take our prayers into consideration?

The Iraq war started when my husband and I were engaged. Without notice, he was off the radar, and I had no idea where he was or when I'd hear from him again. I remember the night the war started, listening to the radio reports of a helicopter downed in the Gulf. The flight had originated from the last place I had heard from him, so of course I assumed the worst.

Prayer, in that wretched moment, seemed like the only possible answer and—at the very same time—a complete and utter mystery to me.

People send their loved ones off to war every day, praying for their safe return, and they never see them again. How do we reconcile such an inconvenient reality? My prayers may not save my husband. So, then, why do they matter?

I turn to the Psalms for some help with these types of questions. The Psalms are some of the rawest prayers in print—particularly Psalm 88. It's an outcry. I love that. And it's questioning the very validity of a prayer life. I love that, too.

Kathleen Norris has a great description of prayer. She sees it as an incessant beginning. Every morning we get up, and our prayer life begins again. We never conquer it, achieve it, complete it. Prayer, she writes, is "being ourselves before God."[3]

I'm trying to embrace this notion of beginning again and again and again. Going back to God, turning toward Him, returning to Him—even as that feels repetitive and unproductive. I'm trying to accept the fact that prayer doesn't move along in a linear fashion, accomplishing as it goes. It moves in a spiral, drilling down into us like a jackhammer tilling up concrete.

Some days I can just manage to breathe in God's direction and somehow, in the sacredness of that unspoken spoken, He breathes back. And, I've found, we can go a long way like that.

Sometimes we wish prayer to be the rudder that changes the course of our entire lives. Yet I wonder if it's our hearts—through the small spokens, the actual truths, the directed breaths—that end up changing. And that's more the point than anything.

Ask

Am I making prayer a part of my life?
Am I able to be honest with God about my
questions and doubts?

Pray

God, I'm willing to pray even though I don't completely understand how it all works. Give me the faith to return to You, each and every day. In Jesus' Name, Amen.

by Bettina Dowell

Treasures OF DARKNESS

I will give you the treasures of darkness, riches stored in secret places, so that you may know that I am the Lord, the God of Israel, who summons you by name.
ISAIAH 45:3

I LIKE TO KEEP my ducks in a row. I am most content when I can get things in my world into ordered little boxes. If these principles are used in my pantry, my bill drawer, or my professional life, they can be powerful tools. However, when I try to fit the journey of my life, or the lives of those I love, into little ordered boxes, we have an instant setup for failure. I have moved from a place of organization, to one of control.

Life as a military spouse demonstrates to us how little control we actually have over our journey. Often the desire to control everything in our spheres of influence (and many things outside of it) springs from a place of fear. Our fear can be born in the tyranny of the "what-ifs?" in life. What if I truly cannot handle the rigors of deployment? What if my spouse endures attacks while he is away from home? What if he never comes home?

So where are we left when we find ourselves trying to control everything due to our fears? Right where God can meet us and show us the treasures of darkness, give us the blessed peace of knowing who is in control, and offer us rest.

Treasures of Darkness: Military life is challenging. Sometimes the journey takes us to some dark places where God desires to teach us. Isaiah 45:3 tells us God will give us riches stored in secrets places, so that we can know He is the Lord.

Peace: No matter what military life brings our way, God is still in control. We can be at peace knowing that nothing is hidden from Him. He has understanding that we cannot fathom, which gives us permission to not have the answers for everything. We can release our control and accept His peace. "Why do you say, O Jacob, and complain, O Israel, 'My way is hidden from the Lord; my cause is disregarded by my God'? Do you not know? Have you not heard? The Lord is the everlasting God, the Creator of the ends of the earth. He will not grow tired or weary, and His understanding no one can fathom" (Isaiah 40:27–28).

Rest: When we decide to trust in our sovereign Father, we open the door to release fear and find the rest that Jesus promised for our souls. Rest for the body is good. Rest for the soul is amazing. "Come to me, all you who are weary and burdened, and I will give you rest" (Matthew 11:28).

As military wives, God longs for us to release our fears, give up control, and learn of the treasures in darkness He has waiting for us.

Ask

Father, what am I truly afraid of in my life?
Where do I need to release control and trust You?

Pray

Thank You, Father, that nothing escapes Your attention. Help me to learn the treasures You have for me in the darkness. In Jesus' Name, Amen.

by Catherine Fitzgerald

Loving THE DIFFICULT ONES

Above all, love each other deeply, because love covers over a multitude of sins.
1 PETER 4:8

AS MILITARY WIVES, we are often in concentrated groups of women. There is so much beauty in the friendships that blossom between women, but sometimes, those blossoms can quickly shrivel when we are confronted with personalities not like our own. It may be an overheard backbiting comment or a conflict over who is to take the lead on a certain event or project. Difficulties in relationships are definitely not unique to military life, but they can certainly be amplified within it.

Our natural, fleshly inclination in response to those tensions that arise in our circles is to strike back. When we butt heads or hear some gossip on what someone has said about us, we are ready in our defense.

Those of us in Christ are held to a higher standard than our immediate knee-jerk-reacting flesh wants us to uphold. Jesus came in order to share this higher standard with us. He said, "But I tell you who hear me: Love your enemies, do good to those who hate you, bless those who curse you, pray for those who mistreat you" (Luke 6:27–28).

We are always on the lookout for the quick solutions to

challenging people in our lives. "Unfriending" them on Facebook, ignoring their calls or deleting their e-mails can seem like a surefire way to handle these individuals. But Christ's words give us a four-step plan that will have not only an earthly return in the relationship, but a heavenly reward as well:

1. Love them: If you don't know what love looks like or how to do it, read through 1 Corinthians 13:4–8.

2. Do good to them: Your mama always said, "Kill 'em with kindness." And guess what—it works! *Do* something nice for them: buy a small gift, send an encouraging note, or offer to babysit their kids.

3. Bless them: Blessings often begin with our tongues. Speak only edifying words about them to others.

4. Pray for them: There is no better antidote to our heart that is hardened against someone who has done us wrong than through praying for them.

I think Christ knew something about us that we so often fail to see. He knew that if we changed our heart, our behaviors, and our prayers, we would undoubtedly see a change in the relationships in our lives. The change would not come because of another's action, but rather our ability through Christ to love in order to cover a multitude of sins, just as He did for us.

Ask

What step do I need to take in loving the difficult person in my life?
How should I be praying for him or her?

Pray

Lord, give me the strength to love, do good, bless, and pray for those I find it hard to love. Help me show grace to others in the same way You have shown grace to me. In Jesus' Name, Amen.

by Leeana Tankersley

RETHINKING MY *Rituals*

I have come that they may have life, and have it to the full.
JOHN 10:10

★ ★ ★

WHEN MY TWINS were ten months old, Steve and I found ourselves moving out of our cramped condo and moving in with my mom—back into the house I grew up in. We wedged our queen-size bed into the 10 x10 bedroom that had once been my little brother's. This was not necessarily my dream scenario.

Right about that time, Steve's job began requiring regular trips to the East Coast. Day after day, I found myself on the floor of my mom's home, exhausted and depressed from solo caretaking, swirling from the toxic voices that invited me to make myself feel better by any means necessary.

Many of us have rituals that we've put into place to help us survive. Some of my least healthy rituals are those that invite me to numb out, vacate my heart and mind, isolate myself, and slip into a soul coma.

Instead of tending to my deeper needs, I plant myself down in front of *The Real Housewives*, and drink an entire case of Diet Coke in a single sitting. Escaping feels good momentarily, but it also tends to backfire, sending me deeper into myself than I was before.

One source of help has been the twelve-step program, Emotions Anonymous (EA), a sister program to AA. EA has helped me identify and surrender my worn-out rituals and begin to build new rituals that help me stay present. EA also encourages me to invite God into the smallest moments of exhaustion and despair, realizing that no situation is too insignificant to say, "Help, Jesus, I'm drowning."

God desires freedom for all of us, a life that is more than numbing and escaping. A full life. We cannot lead a full life if we are constantly looking for ways to flatline our hearts and souls. A full life is born out of the difficult work of asking ourselves questions like:

1. What am I really feeling right now?
2. What do I really need?

If we can identify our true feelings, we can often make healthier decisions about how to care for ourselves. We can begin to think more clearly about what we need. Healthy self-care also involves giving ourselves permission to attend to our true needs. For example: Giving ourselves permission to rest. To cry. To take a night off from the kids. To be imperfect. To get help with my addictive behavior (indulgence or deprivation). To create new rituals.

The full life—the life that is awake and alive—is possible. Take a step toward that life today by inventorying your rituals. Are your coping mechanisms creating light or are they creating darkness?

Ask

Are my rituals destructive or constructive?
Do I know how I'm feeling and what I need in this moment?

Pray

God, I'm scared to relinquish my rituals. I cannot make changes without Your help and Your strength. Please show me the next step I need to take, and give me the courage to take it. In Jesus' Name, Amen.

by Alane Pearce

Whatever!

Finally, brothers and sisters, whatever is true, whatever is noble, whatever is right, whatever is pure, whatever is lovely, whatever is admirable—if anything is excellent or praiseworthy—think about such things.
PHILIPPIANS 4:8

AS MILITARY SPOUSES, we are used to things not going our way. It doesn't mean that we like it, or it gets easier to accept. It's just a fact. After eighteen years as a military spouse, I was a little tired of change and adopted a bad attitude.

I was fortunate to live near my sister for a long tour in Colorado. During our five years there we did a lot together, especially during the holidays. I loved being near family.

When we moved to Texas, just before the holidays, I had a hard time getting into the Christmas spirit. I was frustrated that things wouldn't be the way I was used to them being. I was also still unpacking our household goods and felt displaced. That's when I reached into a box and pulled out a picture frame featuring Philippians 4:8—the "whatever" verse. Surely this was a message for me to turn my thinking around while coping with my frustrations. It was time to refocus and look for some *whatevers* in this season of my life.

God knows what we need for a good, abundant life and he communicated his desire for that in Paul's words. It's not just a saying. There is now scientific evidence that having a positive attitude has a dramatic effect on your health and immunity, your friendships and relationships, your self-esteem, your aging process, and even on your finances. And this is just a short list of the benefits of concentrating on the positive *whatevers* of life.

There's growing evidence that, for many medical illnesses, stress and a negative mental state have a negative effect on immunity. There is also evidence that people who have a positive attitude, or "the fighting spirit," live longer and do better.

There are biblical examples of this principle as well. Paul's life was certainly difficult—having been beaten, shipwrecked, jailed, and left for dead—but he did not focus on his hardships. Rather, he focused on what God was doing in his life: "But one thing I do:" he writes in Philippians, "Forgetting what is behind and straining toward what is ahead, I press on toward the goal to win the prize for which God has called me heavenward in Christ Jesus" (Philippians 3:13–14).

When you find yourself in a circumstance that is not your ideal choice, stop grieving over what isn't. Instead, enjoy what is. Think on the good and seek out that which is worthy of praise. Cherish what is right and true and let go of what makes you frustrated. You just might find that when you look for what is lovely, you'll see it!

Ask

What can I find that is good in the situation I am in? What are the pure, lovely, or praiseworthy aspects of this circumstance?

Prayer

Dear Lord, even though this is not my favorite circumstance, I know that You are still in charge of all things. Help me to accept this; to find the good in it, to find You in it. In Jesus' Name, Amen.

by Pattie Reitz

Vengeance IS THE LORD'S

How long will the enemy mock you, O God?
Will the foe revile your name forever?
PSALM 74:10

WE HAD A PARTICULARLY TRYING PERIOD of attack during my husband's rural church ministry years, and I was angry. We had been wronged, and I wanted revenge. One of our mentors during this time advised us to be careful about how we reacted to the gossip, the lies, and the strife. Above all, he advised, do not seek revenge.

Our country is at war, and in a war there is an enemy. Our enemy wishes harm on us. They use our own words and actions against us to try to win. It is neither friendly, nor fair, nor right. The desire for revenge can become overpowering—and it can eat us alive.

The Bible is clear concerning revenge. Romans 12:19 instructs, "Do not take revenge, my friends, but leave room for God's wrath, for it is written: 'It is mine to avenge; I will repay,' says the Lord." The King James translates it a little bit differently: "'Vengeance is mine,' saith the Lord."

As military wives, sometimes we struggle realizing who our enemy is. Is it the person causing strife with her gossip in church? Is it the Muslim family down the street? Maybe it is the person who cut you off in traffic the other day.

The correct answer is: None of the above. The apostle Paul in Ephesians 6 tells us who our true enemy is: the powers of evil. Satan.

When a war becomes personal, it becomes much harder to avoid the desire for revenge. But oh, my friends, we need to let God seek His own vengeance.

Sometimes it seems like the war has been a part of our lives for so long. And just when it seems things calm down in one locale, another heats up. We send our husbands forth to fight while battling our own wars at home.

Let's not lose sight of who our enemy really is. Yes, our country is at war against terrorists who hate our God and our country and resent our freedom. But our true enemy is evil. And God has already won that war! So let's put on the full armor of God (Ephesians 6:10–18) and remember that our job is not to seek vengeance, but to stand firm.

When the war drags on and our troops are weary, we can look through our eyes of faith and know that God Almighty sees us, knows us, loves us, and has it all under control. "For our struggle is not against flesh and blood, but against the rulers, against the authorities, against the powers of this dark world and against the spiritual forces of evil in the heavenly realms" (Ephesians 6:12).

Ask

How do you deal with battles? How do you combat the struggle against your enemy (fear, discouragement, someone who did wrong to you)?

Pray

Lord, Your Word is clear: Leave revenge to You. I trust You today, and my vengeance is Yours. In Jesus' Name, Amen.

by Sherry Lightner

THE WORK OF *Perseverance*

Consider it pure joy, my brothers and sisters,
whenever you face trials of many kinds, because you know
that the testing of your faith develops perseverance.
Perseverance must finish its work so that you may be
mature and complete, not lacking anything.
JAMES 1:2–5

FOLLOWING THE TERRORIST ATTACKS on September 11, 2001, I realized I was ill-equipped as a military wife. Riveted with fear, I cried out to the Lord. Ten years later, I can see the reflection of God's handprint on my life. He encouraged me, through prayer and His Word, to persevere through each trial and circumstance.

To "persevere" means to maintain a purpose in spite of difficulty, obstacles, or discouragement; in other words, to persist in anything undertaken. As a military wife, our purpose is to support our service member and our family on the home front—and as a child of God, our purpose is to mature in our faith and share the gospel. Both purposes require perseverance because there are obstacles in each path.

"God's goal isn't to make us comfortable here but to help us know him and to intensify our longings for him," Carolyn

Custis James says. "Our troubles are not signs of abandonment but are evidence that he is mightily at work. He uses trouble to draw us closer and open our eyes to see more of him (Hebrews 12:5–11)."[4]

The Bible is full of people who persevered. Nehemiah's prayerful determination allowed God to worked through him, in the midst of discouragement, criticism, and fatigue to rebuild the walls of Jerusalem. As Moses witnessed the Lord's miraculous works—the Lord appearing through flames of fire (Exodus 3:2), the Passover, and the Israelites passing through the Red Sea, Moses was able to persevere.

God desires to use every agonizing trial—a military assignment, raising teenagers, financial strains, or extended family relationships—to strengthen our faith, ultimately preparing us for whatever He has planned for us (Romans 8:28). Even in the midst of our struggles, He desires to mature us through His Word so we would be equipped to persevere in furthering His kingdom.

Ask

Do I have an insatiable desire for God's Word?
Am I willing to be used by God?

Pray

Lord, there are so many times I struggle with ____________________, causing me to be tempted to give up. Yet, through Your Word you continue to encourage me to press on (Philippians 3:14). It is through this pressing, prayer, and Your Word, I have come to know You more intimately with every breath I take. As I persevere through each day, help me to cling to Your Word. Thank You for Your encouragement and for loving me forever. In Jesus' Name, Amen.

by April Lakata Cao

Harvesting THE SOUL

My soul yearns, even faints, for the courts of the Lord; my heart and my flesh cry out for the living God.
PSALM 84:2

★ ★ ★

THE SUMMER FELT LONG and burdensome, in the absence of my husband while I attempt to speed along the ticking clock of another deployment. I began to look forward to fall with its visible passage of time and all of the physical changes ushered in by the season. In the same way that fall is really a beautiful display of a dying-off period I hoped that I, too, would begin to shed the many layers I had built around me in order to survive these past seven months.

In anticipation of my husband's return from Iraq, I needed to begin the process of dying to myself. Like an ear of corn protected beneath the snug, musty green husks, I built a wall to endure outside pressure and temptations; remaining pure and unblemished in thought and spirit. All the while the Lord matured and refined me on the inside, harvesting my soul for the perfect season to reveal a thankful and delighted heart to the man that I love.

Do we wait on the Lord with the same breathless anticipation that comes with a returning spouse, a promotion, or a medical diagnosis? Does our spirit long for the living God as we rise in the morning and continue to yearn for Him into the night (Isaiah 26:9)? Waiting on the Lord is difficult in the midst of trials but James instructs us to, "Consider it pure joy, my brothers and sisters, whenever you face trials of many kinds, because you know that the testing of your faith develops perseverance. Perseverance must finish its work so that you may be mature and complete, not lacking anything" (James 1:2–4).

Like a field being prepared for planting God does not waste the elements needed to refine us while we wait on Him (Psalm 66:10). If we, as God's children, are devoid of patience, compassion, and humility, then we will fail to grow and nurture a relationship with Him. Soil, while tilled and turned year after year, contains the life blood necessary to nourish new seeds. Good seeds must be viable in order to grow and produce fruit. Our faith is alive, calling us into action by trusting, praying, and repenting (Matthew 3:8). While fruit is fragile, always at the mercy of the weather, God is our permanent shelter from the storm. The fruit He produces in us can mature and thrive even while withstanding the harshest conditions. Anticipate the Lord by seeking Him daily (Proverbs 3:6). Praise Him in humble thanksgiving, acknowledging every blessing so that in our troubles we are already yoked with Christ, awaiting the next harvest.

Do I excitedly anticipate the Lord in my comings and goings?
Do I put into practice living faith in order to grow and mature?

Lord, use every moment to shape and refine me for Your good purposes. I long to be in Your presence. Help me to abide in Your Word daily so that I may grow in truth and obedience. Let my soul produce sweet fruit so that I am ready for the harvest. In Jesus' Name, Amen.

Section Two

INTIMATE ALLIES:

Protecting Your Military Marriage

Therefore what God has joined together, let no one separate.

MARK 10:9

by Alane Pearce

Committed

So they are no longer two, but one flesh.
Therefore what God has joined together, let no one separate.
MATTHEW 19:6

MY HUSBAND IS AIR FORCE, which means his deployments are short and infrequent. Or they were. Until one particular time when during two and a half years I saw him for about 120 days between his deployments and TDYs.

To manage, I went on trips and threw myself into work. He worked long days immersed in his job, and we stopped having things in common. He couldn't share with me what he was doing because it was highly classified. We began living parallel lives and forgot how to be spouses.

During e-mail and weekly phone calls, we hit the high points: "Corbin got As on his report card." "I'm going out in the field tomorrow." We were merely high-fiving as we passed each other in our lives. We were no longer one, but two.

This is one of the risks of a military marriage—and the reason why we should be even more vigilant to keep our marriage vows of "for better or for worse." The military lifestyle can cause extreme strain on marriages.

God is serious about marriage, and it takes a daily commitment to make marriage work—even in the good times. When you are separated due to deployment, it takes even more work. Wars and deployments threaten to tear us apart—but God said, let no one separate what God has joined together.

To help your marriage survive the stresses of deployments, consider these ideas:

- Write "snail mail" letters to your warrior telling him why he's so important to you and how much you love him. Don't mention the day-to-day in these letters but use them to reconnect with the love you share.
- Make sure you date. It allows you to reconnect as a couple. If you are apart, set up a Skype date. Dress to impress him. Think of clever stories or questions to add a new spark to your conversations.
- Take time for the two of you every day when he is home. After the kids are in bed, turn off the television and talk. Ask questions. Reconnect. This time will renew your friendship and give you some common experiences.

You made a vow to love and care for each other for as long as you live. When you make a point to commit to your marriage each day—because God said to—you will find that even when you are separated during a deployment, you can maintain a strong relationship. It takes hard work, but my husband and I can both attest that it is well worth the effort.

Ask

In what new way can I commit to my marriage today? How can I connect with my spouse while he is deployed?

Pray

Father, You have joined my husband and me together, and I don't want anything to tear us apart. Please show me how I can love my husband to honor You and improve our relationship. In Jesus' Name, Amen.

by Jocelyn Green

Predeployment DISTANCE

He withdrew about a stone's throw beyond them,
knelt down and prayed.
LUKE 22:41

"NOW THAT MY HUSBAND is about to deploy, it's like there's a brick wall between us," a woman wrote to me in an e-mail. "We can't seem to connect on anything!"

Military wives for generations have experienced predeployment (or TDY) emotional distancing. Tensions are high as couples anticipate the upcoming deployment in different ways; conditions are ripe for arguments and harsh words. It isn't fun, but it is normal.

Books and seminars explain what predeployment detachment is all about. But I'd like to bring your attention to a different source: Luke 22:39–46. On the night of Jesus' betrayal just prior to His crucifixion, He and His disciples went to the Mount of Olives. But when He reached a certain point, He told them to stay and pray, while He withdrew (see verse 41). Here's what I noticed in this passage:

1. **Jesus withdrew.** He required the time and space to mentally and spiritually prepare for the task. When a soldier withdraws before a separation from his family, he also does it to focus.

2. **The disciples didn't understand.** The disciples loved Jesus and were sorrowful that He would be leaving them soon (verse 45), but there was no way they could fully comprehend what was about to happen. Unless we were once active-duty military, we just can't fathom the stresses our military men are under.

3. **Jesus still wanted support.** Jesus had the disciples accompany Him to a certain point. Your husband still wants your love and support too, even if he's withdrawn. Support him through prayer and by helping with whatever he needs to get done before he goes. Write love notes and tuck them into his luggage.

Just as Jesus was preparing for His ultimate purpose of crucifixion and resurrection, your husband is preparing to fulfill his vocational purpose, as well.

Marine wife Jan Hamme says, "As we prepared for deployment, I reminded myself that my husband would be doing what he had been training to do. He was even excited about it! I had to be sure to not resent that excitement or he would have to hide his feelings from me. I knew he would miss me, but he was still a Marine, going about the work he had chosen and God had called him to do!"

If you find yourself struggling with your husband's emotional detachment or withdrawal, cling instead to God's love. As Sara Horn says in *Tour of Duty*, "Don't take your husband's behavior personally. Instead, take the opportunity to show love to him, the way God shows love to all of us. Unconditionally."[1]

What can I do to show my support of my husband this week?
How can I cling to God's love for my own support?

Lord, please help me guard my expectations of my husband during this period so I don't set myself up for disappointment. Show me how to love him with Your love. In Jesus' Name, Amen.

by April Lakata Cao

PERFECTION IN *Marriage*

And over all these virtues put on love,
which binds them all together in perfect unity.
COLOSSIANS 3:14

★ ★ ★

TWELVE YEARS AGO I married a man whom I thought epitomized perfection, and somewhere along the way I decided he was perfect enough for the both of us. And then later, when life did not go my way, I resented him for not being the man I thought I needed. The golden pedestal I had placed him on slowly began to tarnish and crumble as the grief of infertility, separation, and loneliness took root in my heart. Thankfully, God used our sixth move to a nondeployable duty station to shake me from my complacency.

I finally understood that my problem with perfection had nothing to do with my husband and everything to do with me. I had to stop blaming the military for my unhappiness and take responsibility for my part of the chaos. While I yearned for my spouse to fulfill the desires of my heart, I had a Father in heaven who wanted to gloriously fulfill each and every need (Philippians 4:19). Instead of relying on God's Word to direct my thoughts and attitude I allowed my sinful, human nature to shape the way I gave and received love.

There is no better example of perfect, agape love than God's gift to us through His Son Jesus. "But God demonstrates his own love for us in this: While we were still sinners, Christ died for us" (Romans 5:8). Jesus walked among us as the embodiment of pure, sinless, and unfailing love in order to exemplify the full measure and character of God. Just as Jesus did not have to die for us but wanted to out of perfect love and obedience, we should want to love and care for our spouse so we may bring honor and glory to God. We are not commanded to love only when given an assurance of love in return, but "as I have loved you, so you must lovc onc another" (John 13:34b).

The healing process can begin by approaching your spouse and asking forgiveness for any action or attitude that has been unloving or disrespectful (1 John 1:9). In turn, forgive your spouse for any past hurts so that you may be released from the bondage of bitterness (Matthew 6:15). The next time you're tempted to find fault with your spouse, take a moment in thankful prayer for his many positive attributes. Are your words building up and encouraging your spouse according to his needs (Ephesians 4:29)? Remember that God created marriage not just for our happiness but for His holiness and that it is perfect when He is in it.

Ask

Is the love I have for my spouse conditional
and guided by my emotions?
Do I demonstrate love that is quick to listen and slow to speak?

Pray

Lord, help me to be a wife who desires a humble and obedient heart. Teach me to love my husband even when I feel his actions are unlovable. Conform my heart and actions to be in perfect harmony with Your will as I strive to demonstrate agape love. Thank You for the blessing of my husband. In Jesus' Name, Amen.

by Jocelyn Green

TO LOVE LIKE *Christ*

But God demonstrates his own love for us in this:
While we were still sinners, Christ died for us.
ROMANS 5:8

WHEN MY COAST GUARD officer fiancé (now my husband) told me he was scheduled to go to New Zealand for several weeks, my heart sank.

"I'm afraid you'll go and realize you don't need me after all," I confessed.

"I don't need you," he said without missing a beat. I was stunned.

"But life is just so much better with you," he quickly added.

With that simple statement, Rob summed up a truth of military marriage that we see paralleled in God's love for us, as well.

Romans 5:8 says, "But God demonstrates his own love for us in this: While we were still sinners, Christ died for us." While many relationships in today's society are transactional—i.e., "I love you because of what you do for me"—God's love for us has nothing to do with what He gets from us. He doesn't need us to make Him feel good or to accomplish His purposes (but He does graciously allow us to participate in His work). The closer we can come to reflecting that kind of selfless love to our spouse, the more we understand the nature of Christ's love for the church.

There is a scene in *The Great Divorce* by C. S. Lewis where a couple who had been married on earth is reunited in heaven. The woman, who had reached heaven first, says to her former husband, "[On earth] I loved you for my own sake: because I needed you . . . I am full now, not empty. I am in Love Himself, not lonely. Strong, not weak. . . . We shall have no *need* for one another now: we can begin to love truly."[2]

When we are full of God's love, we can love our husbands with fewer demands on them to meet our emotional needs. "One true blessing of living this life where deployments are the norm, is that we are faced continually with the surprising reality that we are strong enough to live life on our own, but because of love, we choose not to," says Army wife Jill Bozeman. "Loving someone because you *need* them is selfish love, but loving someone because you choose to is *true* love."

We can also discover a greater depth to God's love by looking at the military marriage. The heartache we feel for our absent spouse is what God feels when we, His bride, break fellowship with Him as well. He cares about being with us so much that He sent Jesus to earth to restore that fellowship with us. Jesus' name Immanuel means *God with us* (Matthew 1:23). The next time you long for your husband's presence, realize that you have a unique glimpse into God's heart as He feels that same longing to be in fellowship with you!

Ask

What am I trying to get from my husband
that only God can give me?
How can I draw closer to the Lord this week?

Pray

Lord, I praise You for loving me fully and completely. Help me find satisfaction in Your love so I can more freely love my husband. In Jesus' Name, Amen.

by Linda Montgomery

THE SUBMARINER *Treatment*

A man reaps what he sows.
GALATIANS 6:7

WHEN OUR SUBMARINERS are preparing to go underway, they are given an extensive dental screening to identify and treat any potential problems. This at one time was referred to by some as "The Submariner Treatment." It may sound radical, but eliminating risk is serious business.

What if we gave our marriages "The Submariner Treatment" before deployment?

The Bible tells us that we will reap what we sow (Galatians 6:7). Whatever seeds of trust, commitment, and love we can plant in our marriages today, we can nurture and reap a harvest of intimacy. We need to pull any weeds from our relationships (e.g., bitterness, suspicion, jealousy) that could possibly threaten to choke out what is good and healthy in our marriages. When preparing for a separation, doing our best to "eliminate risk" in the realm of marriage is critical.

Consider the following suggestions:

- Identify some issues that had not been dealt with in your marriage before they get worse from the stress of separation

- Read a book on good communication skills in marriage, and discuss it
- Be open to something radical—like eliminating a friendship that has a negative influence
- Decide, ahead of time, what would be the best way to spend R&R (away, or at home; in-laws, or no in-laws)
- Talk about expectations and fears
- Make sure that the one at home is "plugged in" to a good support network
- Be sure that the maintenance on the car and house (and computer) are up-to-date; plan for emergencies
- Invite a couple with deployment experience over for dinner so that you can discuss some of the unexpected challenges
- Learn to pray together and renew your commitment to love each other sacrificially.

But what if problems were not addressed before deployment, and now they're even worse? Unlike the situation of a submariner underway with a toothache and no help, God is always present and available—there is no problem too large or too small for His care.

Ask

What can you do, as a couple, to prepare for the time apart—in hopes of avoiding problems? If you are already separated by distance, what can you do this week to demonstrate your love for and commitment to your spouse?

Pray

Lord, I know that You believe in our marriage and want my husband and me to grow closer to each other no matter where we are. Please give us the desire and discipline to work on our relationship before, during, and after separations. In Jesus' Name, Amen.

by Claire Shackelford

THE POWERFUL ACT OF *Submission*

Wives, submit yourselves to your own husbands as you do to the Lord.
EPHESIANS 5:22

★ ★ ★

A MARRIAGE IS STRONG when it is built with Jesus as the sure Foundation and Master Builder. Labors of love are the bricks, and sacrifice is the mortar that binds it together. Sinful pride and self-centeredness are often the "wrecking ball" to even the strongest marriage.

Bad storms, such as constant deployments, training, and other life stresses, can't take down a building built on a sure foundation, but a wrecking ball, on the other hand, is created for demolition!

Submission is a vital part of our walk with the Lord. It is a tool in our sanctification as it helps us to let go of our sinful pride and "self." We are given a wonderful opportunity to practice a high level of submission in marriage.[3]

The world tells us that submission is weakness and is used to subjugate women, but in reality as wives we hold a lot of power. Any person in a position of headship, leadership, or power can be made or broken by the people he or she leads.

Consider the story of Moses and the Israelites in Numbers

chapter 20, for example. When Moses led the Israelites he met a lot of opposition through grumbling. Moses was a good leader, but the Israelites were not good followers. They followed Moses, but they did not submit themselves fully by trusting him and trusting the Lord.

When Moses is asked to provide water (a task the Lord had done through him before) the Israelites tempt Moses through their complaining. The result was disastrous. The lack of faith displayed through the complaining brought Moses to anger, and in turn caused him to stumble and sin. Because of this, Moses and Aaron both were told they would not lead the people into the Promised Land.

Moses and Aaron reaped the responsibility of their own sin, but the Israelites can certainly share in the blame. This is a convicting point when we each pause to reflect on our "followship" as disciples of Christ, wives, mothers, sisters, daughters, and citizens.

Jesus submitted Himself fully and perfectly to the will of the Father, and it accomplished our salvation! Submission is not a passive and weak characteristic trait, but a partnership designed by God to accomplish His purposes.

Ask

What kind of a follower am I? Do I joyfully submit to godly leadership? Do I see submission as a blessing?

Pray

Lord Jesus, thank You for Your perfect submission to the Father's will, even unto death. Please forgive ME as I fall short, and help me as I strive to submit to You and to the leadership You have placed over me. In Jesus' Name, Amen.

by April Lakata Cao

Communicating EXPECTATIONS

And they did not do as we expected, but they gave themselves first to the Lord and then to us in keeping with God's will.
2 CORINTHIANS 8:5

★ ★ ★

AFTER MULTIPLE MOVES, deployments, and the birth of our first child without my husband present, the disappointment from my shattered expectations began to take a toll on our marriage. I became disillusioned and then later resentful because, according to my feelings, my husband had not met my needs. I imagine that if we all took an honest look at the root cause of our marital conflicts we'd come to the conclusion that, more often than not, they stem from miscommunicated or unspoken expectations.

The problem with expectations is that they are shaped by human emotion, and emotions can easily deceive us. It is imperative, when learning to adjust our expectations, to base them on the truth that is the Word. Consider the Macedonian church who, despite their severe affliction, joyfully made Christ their first priority. They did not despair in their circumstances but exceeded Paul's expectations of generosity. We, too, can exceed the expectations of our spouse by imparting honor and respect while first faithfully serving God. Practically speaking, if what we feel becomes our gauge for how we act, then what we believe becomes conditional. If we believe, through faith, that the Lord is sovereign (Isaiah 55:9) then we will define our expectations according to His will.

Once we have aligned ourselves with God's instruction and commit to submitting ourselves to His authority, how do we then approach communication with our spouse? First, we must use our words to encourage and edify (Ephesians 4:29).

Second, we must effectively and fairly communicate our expectations. Whether it's about finances, parenting, or intimacy, our words should be designed to encourage a godly response from our helpmate. Godly direction requires us to be gentle and thoughtful, not overbearing and argumentative. Remember, we are not using our words to solicit the response we're hoping to get. Our goal is not to manipulate but to encourage intimacy and a godly reaction from our spouse.

Lastly, how will we respond to a spouse who does not give us the answer or reaction we are looking for even when we communicate effectively? "Everyone should be quick to listen, slow to speak and slow to become angry" (James 1:19). Our emotions can easily get the best of us when we don't hear what we want, and this is where conflict happens. Take the time to consider your spouse's point of view. The goal is not to be right, but to understand each other, and to honor God through the process.

Ask

Do I communicate my expectations clearly? Are my expectations based on God's truth and not my own emotions?

Pray

Heavenly Father, help me to better communicate my expectations to (your spouse's name). I want to honor You and my husband with my words. I no longer desire to be led by my emotions, but guided by Your desires for my marriage. In Jesus' Name, Amen.

by Jocelyn Green

"HE Owes ME"

[Love] is not self-seeking, it is not easily angered, it keeps no record of wrongs.
1 CORINTHIANS 13:5

WHEN HER HUSBAND'S WEEKS at sea dragged on during his first long trip of their marriage, Coast Guard wife Karen Whiting turned to another "Coastie" wife to commiserate.

"I've counted the days we've been together and apart. The days apart outnumber the days together," the other wife spat. "He owes me a lot."

Remembering 1 Corinthians 13:5—"Love keeps no record of wrongs"—Karen immediately resolved not to follow in this bitter woman's footsteps. She thought, "I do *not* want a negative attitude. I won't count the days. It will not help our children, our relationship, or me. Besides, Jim misses us too."

Today, Karen and her husband have weathered twenty-two years in the military together. The other woman in the story divorced her husband long ago.

I imagine we have all resented our husbands' absences at one time or another. It is natural to miss your spouse when he's away, but beware when that turns to anger, causing you to blame him for the military's schedule for him. A sense of entitlement can crop up in even the most unsuspecting hearts, whispering seductively: *You deserve better than this. He owes you!* When those thoughts arise, put them on trial and cross-examine them! Nancy Leigh DeMoss says it well:

> If we as women focus on what we "deserve," on our "rights," or on what men "ought" to do for us, we will become vulnerable to hurt and resentment when our expectations are not fulfilled. Blessing and joy are the fruit of seeking to be a giver rather than a taker and of looking for ways to bless, serve, and minster to the needs of our families.[4]

First Peter 5:5–6 puts it this way: "All of you, clothe yourselves with humility toward one another, because, 'God opposes the proud but gives grace to the humble.' Humble yourselves, therefore, under God's mighty hand, that he may lift you up in due time."

The idea of clothing ourselves with humility (verse 5) seems to imply:

1. We weren't born with it, so we need to deliberately put on humility.
2. We should do it daily.
3. If we don't clothe ourselves with humility, we will be exposed and vulnerable to the sin of pride (and entitlement).

When we clothe ourselves with humility, our love will simply have no reason to keep record of wrongs against us—real or imagined. Karen says, "We cannot easily change our lifestyle, but we can adjust our attitudes."

Ask

Do I use my husband's frequent absences as leverage against him? How can I demonstrate humility in my marriage this week?

Pray

Lord, give me the grace, humility, and strength to not keep score when I feel wronged by my husband. Keep my eyes focused on You, Lord, as my ultimate example of humility. In Jesus' Name, Amen.

by Linda Montgomery

Loving WITHOUT SEEING

"Now faith is being sure of what we hope for and certain of what we do not see."
HEBREWS 11:1

A NAVY FRIEND OF OURS went underway shortly after his wedding, aboard a submarine that didn't allow for any e-mail, telephone calls, letters, or texting. So to bridge the distance, this young couple had decided to each "share" their thoughts throughout the months apart by recording them in journals.

Perhaps a married couple experiencing deployment is the closest picture of a Christian's faith. Just as she had to believe that he existed—somewhere in the sea—she had to trust his character and have hope in his promised return. She had to believe that when she was "communicating" with him by writing daily in her journal that he cared about what she was going through—and loved her deeply. The same was true with him. The journal was a daily routine with an unseen wife whom he counted on to believe in him. The oneness in their Christian marriage grew.

Doesn't that sound like what we do as Christians? We have faith in an unseen God. We know His character, we know that He loves us, and we trust Him to forgive us and care about us as we grow in grace. We know that He wants to hear from us in prayer—to hear what we are thinking, feeling, and learning from His Word. We know that He has promised to return, and we cling to that promise. We know that life as we see it now is only a foretaste of life to come and we have hope.

Communication studies teach us that as a couple grows in oneness they will trust each other more. They will learn to share more than just information, opinions, and emotions, and will actually grow closer by seeking to understand and be understood. They will be transparent with each other enough to share the other's hopes, dreams, lessons learned, fears, needs, beliefs, struggles, disappointments, prayers, and understandings of who God is personally. The oneness that they always hoped for can be real—perhaps through the struggle to survive the deployment.

In the same way, while we are apart from our heavenly Bridegroom, we can still nurture a close, personal relationship with Him by pouring our hearts out to Him (Psalm 62:8) and by reading what He wrote to us in His Word. We can meditate on and trust in His precious promises: He loves you (Psalm 90:14); He is with you (Psalm 139:7–10); He is faithful (Psalm 145:13); He is your comforter (2 Corinthians 1:3), your help, and your shield (Psalm 33:20–22). He has a plan for your life, and it is good (Jeremiah 29:11).

Ask

How can you move your level of communication with your spouse to a deeper level this week?
Which of God's promises in Scripture are especially comforting to you right now? Memorize those verses.

Pray

Lord, thank You for Your Word, which tells us of Your love and provision for us even though we won't see You face-to-face until we meet in heaven. Give me the desire to invest in meaningful communication with my spouse, but even more so with You. In Jesus' Name, Amen.

by April Lakata Cao

HOLINESS BEFORE *Happiness*

And he died for all, that those who live should no longer live for themselves but for him who died for them and was raised again.
2 CORINTHIANS 5:15

THE SEVENTEENTH-CENTURY Christian writer Francis de Sales described marriage as one of the most difficult ministries a person could undertake: "The state of marriage is one that requires more virtue and consistency than any other."[5] In his book *Sacred Marriage*, Gary Thomas asks, "What if God designed marriage to make us holy more than to make us happy?"[6]

If the God of the universe created marriage for much more than our happiness then it strikes a blow to contemporary society's infatuation with romantic love and requires us, as Christians, to examine our relationship beyond superficial expectations. A Christ-centered marriage drives us to bring glory to God. And if pleasing God is our motivation, if following the gospels becomes our singular purpose, then we have already taken the first step toward holiness.

How do we begin to make holiness a priority in our marriage? The answer lies within God's design of marriage to shift us from an internal to an eternal perspective, naturally drawing us into closer relationship with Him. First, marriage exposes our sins. Being in partnership casts a bright light on shortcomings and sin that can be devastating to our spiritual growth. Having someone to lovingly rebuke us (Matthew 18:15) in the face of our weakness encourages repentance. Second, marriage teaches one of the most difficult spiritual disciplines: forgiveness. Withholding forgiveness from our spouse separates us from the love of God (Mark 11:25). Forgiving an unkindness without qualifiers reminds us that, in spite of our unworthiness, we were forgiven of our sins (Romans 5:6–10).

Lastly, marriage teaches us to seek, practice, and participate in reconciliation. Our marriage covenant is like the analogy of God's union with Israel and later between Christ and the Church, and it is an outward reflection of our divine relationship between God and His people (Ephesians 5:25–27). By pursuing reconciliation with our spouse we are inviting God to faithfully restore, heal, and renew what we have broken.

The Lord is clear that He desires us to be happy but that our joy should be drawn "from the wells of salvation" (Isaiah 12:3), not from our flesh. Through the gift of marriage we are free to pursue holiness while experiencing love, intimacy, and pleasure.

Is the pursuit of holiness a priority in my marriage? Do I allow conflict to draw me into closer relationship with God?

Dear God, I want my happiness to come from a deep and fulfilling relationship with You. Help me to have an eternal perspective and give me a joyful heart that desires to serve my husband in all circumstances. Thank You for my marriage, which draws me closer to You! In Jesus' Name, Amen.

by Sharon Carrns

MORE THAN A CONSTANT *Dripping*

A quarrelsome wife is like the constant dripping of a leaky roof.
PROVERBS 19:13B

★ ★ ★

WHEN MY HUSBAND AND I were dating I continued working on my career in Austin, Texas. Only one time did he go to the field for a couple of weeks in the year before he proposed marriage.

Later we moved to Fort Knox. I discovered that the small town outside Fort Knox was no Austin. Opportunities like the ones I had before becoming a military wife were few. The culture shock hit me full force. Even getting my ID card was hard for me. The person taking the information called me a *dependent*, saying my husband's information was all that mattered. I had depended on no one, working my way through college and up through the corporate ranks.

When his course at Fort Knox was finished we moved to Fort Carson. Now real training and deployments began. John was gone half of all our time there. I became more and more bitter. As a quarrelsome wife I nagged at my husband like a constant dripping. I wanted out of this life and back to one where I thought we both mattered. My heart and mind needed understanding—and adjusting. Volunteering at Army Community Service help me do both.

If you feel your life doesn't matter next to that of your military spouse, you are not alone. Lots of us have felt that way. Many of us have been able to *find our way* again by reevaluating the places where we might find fulfillment and feelings of worth.

A wise wife told me, "Your time will come. This is only one season." There are many ways you are needed and important in this season of your military life together. Seek ways to help you feel valued. A "constant dripping" of negativity will make *both* you and your spouse miserable.

As you work through these feelings, consider who you are serving. Colossians 3:23–24 says, "Whatever you do, work at it with all your heart, as working for the Lord, not for men, since you know that you will receive an inheritance from the Lord as a reward. It is the Lord Christ you are serving."

Will you struggle with feelings? Yes. But it does help keep a perspective. And Jesus values your worth above all others.

Deciding to stop dripping and start pouring out my heart and talents for God, my marriage, and others gave me deep joy. It can give you the same.

Ask

Am I a partner to my husband or a constant dripping of bitterness and complaints?
Are there other ways to find joy and meaning in my life as a military wife that I haven't considered?

Pray

Father God, Your plan for me may be different than the plans I had anticipated for myself. But I ask You to show me Your plan. I know I will find meaning and worth in it. In Jesus' Name, Amen.

by Marshéle Carter Waddell

THE PATH TO *Infidelity*

But this I call to mind, and therefore I have hope: The steadfast love of the Lord never ceases; his mercies never come to an end; they are new every morning; great is your faithfulness.
LAMENTATIONS 3:21–23 ESV

THE STORY OF BATHSHEBA is familiar to most of us. King David saw this beautiful woman, the wife of a warrior on a combat deployment. He desired her, and the king usually got what he wanted. The Bible doesn't tell us much about Bathsheba's intent in this drama, which you can read about in 2 Samuel 11.

Centuries earlier, Potiphar's wife knew what she wanted—Joseph (Genesis 39:7–12). We don't know what this military wife's motives were; perhaps it was that Joseph was young, good-looking, and desirable. And perhaps Potiphar wasn't, or maybe he was often absent or inattentive when he was present. Whatever his wife's thinking was, she was reaching out for something that didn't belong to her.

Military wives can relate to both beautiful Bathsheba and pitiful Mrs. Potiphar. We work hard, wait long, and wonder how to stoke the flames of marital love and passion, cooled by years of selfless service and months, even years, of being apart. The stress of extended and more frequent wartime deployments, single parenting, fear, and fatigue threaten to suffocate the last, struggling embers of what once was our undying passion for our men.

A work relationship unexpectedly develops into more than just business. We go online out of late night boredom and, surprise, we find a soul mate in cyberspace. We've waited weeks to hear from hubby. Our virtual friend responds in seconds.

It's innocent. We're just friends, we rationalize. Suddenly, we realize the relationship is sexually charged. Dizzied, we stand at the edge. We consider leaping. The future balances precariously between what is and what could be. We try to convince ourselves that the leap will be an exhilarating flight, not a deadly free fall.

The emotional void and physical vacancy caused by the demands of military life leave us hungry for connection, conversation, and companionship. The choice is ours. The temptation is present daily in the lives of military wives. An affair is a real experience or a real possibility we've all considered and a powerful lure for the tired, burned out, and lonely ones on the home front.

We've all been unfaithful to some degree. We've all wrestled with affairs of the heart, if not of the flesh. We must choose faithfulness daily, hourly, sometimes in five-minute intervals.

Where do I struggle with unfaithfulness?
How can I avoid the temptation—whether it's an affair of the heart or the flesh—altogether?

Father, thank You that You are a gracious and loving God, compassionate and slow to anger. Lord, nothing is hidden from You. You are fully aware of my infidelities of the flesh and of the heart. I confess my adultery to you and ask for Your forgiveness. Thank You that though others condemn me, You do not. Thank You that Your mercies are new every morning. Help me, Father, to live a life worthy of You and to please You in every way. Thank You that I am blameless in Your sight because I am in Christ Your Son. In Jesus' Name, Amen.

by Rosie Williams

NOT THE MAN I *Married*

But the wisdom that comes from heaven is first of all pure; then peace-loving, considerate, submissive, full of mercy and good fruit, impartial and sincere.
JAMES 3:17

I OFTEN HEAR military wives say "my husband was not the man I married" after deployment. My husband was a combat infantryman in Vietnam, wounded both physically and invisibly. Having married shortly after he returned, I could definitely see changes. I sought God for wisdom, and years later learned about post-traumatic stress disorder (PTSD). Still, he is the same guy I committed to in sickness and in health forty years ago.

PTSD affects everyone differently, and may take years to surface. When your spouse was deployed, he had a mission. Once he is home, you too have a mission: to love him through the transition back home. If your spouse has PTSD, it will take patience and wisdom as you take this journey together. Here's what I've learned:

- Although some of his reactions and attitudes have changed, there is hope for healing over time.
- Seek God's wisdom to know how to deal not only with his wounds, but also with yours.
- If he processes his experience by telling war stories over and over . . . listen over and over. When he repeats he is dealing with powerful emotions. The well of grief may

be so deep, healing could take years.

- If he withdraws, he may be trying to protect you from haunting details. In time, he may share, but pressuring him may cause further withdrawal. Encourage him to share with other vets.
- If memories cause him to be anxious or depressed, he may not be able to verbalize why he is feeling or acting a certain way. By educating yourself about PTSD and meeting with others who are going through the same thing, you will gain much support.

When you think about him being different from "the man you married," consider the positive. The man you married may have been immature and idealistic. The man who returned has been tested by fire, has more maturity, strength, knowledge, and understanding. His faith may be deeper and more authentic. Imagine looking at him within a frame of who he is becoming as he processes his experiences. If you let your commitment carry you through tough times, your love and respect will help him transition home.

Note: If your spouse is abusive to you or other family members, it is important to seek professional help. Lovingly encourage him to go too, but realize you may need to take the first step.

Ask

Why do you think it is hard for couples to ask for help?
How is wisdom described in James 3:17?

Pray

Lord, as my marriage changes, change me too. Show me how to love as You love. I pray that You would heal the physical and emotional wounds we have experienced. In Jesus' Name, Amen.

by Sarah Ball

TWO ARE BETTER THAN *One*

Two are better than one, because they have
a good return for their work:
If one falls down, his friend can help him up . . .
A cord of three strands is not quickly broken.
ECCLESIASTES 4:9–10, 12

"HONEY, I'M NOT REALLY HUNGRY YET. Could we wait a little while to have dinner?" my husband asked.

"If we don't have dinner at 5:30, then I won't have time clean up the kitchen, give the kids baths, read them stories, and get them to bed on time," I explained. My husband had only been home from deployment for a few days, so he obviously didn't understand the family schedule just yet.

"But I could clean up the kitchen while you give them baths, or I could give them baths and read them stories. I'm just sitting here watching you do everything all the time."

He was right. During deployment, I became very independent. I parented our daughter, gave birth to our son, ran the house, maintained the cars, mowed the lawn, and did everything on schedule. My strategy for coping with the separation was to carry out my husband's roles as well as my own. When he came home, I wasn't ready to return those roles to him. He'd probably mess up my routines. He might put things away in the wrong places, or dress the kids in mismatched clothes.

Like many military spouses, I have learned how to be

independent and even thrive when my husband is gone. The difficulty comes when he returns to his place in our home and family. I could give him back the responsibilities around the house, but I know he may leave again. Each deployment ends with a new struggle for me to allow him back into the center of our family life and the roles that God intends for him to have.

Our marriage began with verses from Ecclesiastes 4:9–12. My husband and I braided a cord of three strands during our wedding. We wanted to show that we would be united as husband and wife in Christ, and that God would hold our marriage together and keep us strong. Wc had no idea then of the deployments that would stretch our strand of three cords around the world for years at a time.

We cannot prevent the times when our marriages are geographically stretched. The only control we have is over our own response to the challenge. Remember the promise that you made before God to be united to your husband. Choose to embrace him fully when he returns home. Let him lead your family, parent your children, and be your husband and best friend. As two, you are better than you could ever be on your own. And your cord of three strands will not easily be broken.

Ask

Have I committed myself completely to unity
in my marriage before God?
Am I allowing my husband to be an active leader
and parent in our home?

Pray

Dear Lord, thank You for the husband You have given me. Draw us into greater unity in our marriage with You as the center. Show me how to transition between separations and homecomings, always seeking a marriage and home that honor You. In Jesus' Name, Amen.

Section Three

TOUR OF DUTY:

Overcoming Deployments and Other Separations

They will have no fear of bad news; their hearts are steadfast, trusting in the Lord.

PSALM 112:7

by Sarah Ball

MORE THAN *Surviving*

He has showed you, O man, what is good.
And what does the Lord require of you? To act justly and to love mercy and to walk humbly with your God.
MICAH 6:8

I SPENT MY HUSBAND'S first deployment just trying to hang on—drawing strength from Scripture and asking God to get me through the next hour or two of the day. I read the Psalms over and over and wrote "The Deployment" next to certain psalms that gave me encouragement and peace.

At some point, I came to a very disturbing realization. My husband began talking about the "next" deployment before he had even returned from his first one, and I realized that "The Deployment" was just the first of an unknown number. I had to start asking myself some tough questions.

Do I want to spend my life just surviving deployments? Or does God have a greater purpose for me during these tough times? As my husband's second and then third deployments arrived, I began to see that God wanted to teach me much more than just surviving.

Micah 6:8 poetically summarizes God's purpose for each of us. Acting justly and loving mercy are both directed at the people around us, so God is directing us toward ministry to others. Walking humbly with God is a reminder that we need an ongoing relationship with God to guide us. Simply put, God asks us to do two things: Worship God and serve others.

Worship and service can determine whether a deployment year is filled with painful survival or growth and purpose. As we worship God, we receive strength and peace to get through difficulty, but we also gain much more. We see God carry us through hardships, and we grow in confidence in our God. We aren't tempted to be proud of our own personal strength and independence, because we know where the glory belongs.

As we walk humbly with God, we are prepared to serve others. Opportunities for simple kindness are all around us—a smile for a tired cashier or a few encouraging words to a lonely neighbor require only a little thought on our part. Intentional moments of service to others can take our focus off our own stress. During one of our hardest deployments, I carefully scheduled one act of service into each week, an extra act of kindness beyond my normal activities. That allowed me to look back at the end of each week and say to myself, "Look, this week wasn't just about you and your hard times."

If you are slogging through deployment days right now, I challenge you to do more than just survive. Choose to worship God. Choose to serve others. People will be encouraged, God will be glorified, and you will receive the most benefit as you grow in character and love for God.

Ask

What purpose does God have for me at this time in my life?
How can I offer service to someone near me today?

Pray

Dear Lord, You have called me to walk humbly with You through all the challenges of military life. Please give me strength for the challenges of today and a heart that worships You. Grant me opportunities to serve others in Your name. In Jesus' Name, Amen.

by Jocelyn Green

FINDING *Joy*

A cheerful heart is good medicine,
but a crushed spirit dries up the bones.
PROVERBS 17:22

★ ★ ★

I HELD THE MENU in front of my eyes and stared at it, unseeing. My new husband had gone to sea that morning for the first of many separations, and these women invited me to dine with them. Still, I brooded.

"Get the Caesar." The captain's wife interrupted my gloomy reverie. "No one will care your breath smells like garlic for the rest of the night. I always get the Caesar salad when Jay is underway."

She had a great point! I will always remember that moment as the time when I began to learn that living life as a military wife doesn't mean waiting until your husband comes home to experience joy, but finding it wherever you can, and relishing it, just as I absolutely relished that Caesar salad that night.

The point is not that we wait until our husbands leave to have a lot of fun. More importantly, we recognize that there is joy in life—all of it—not just the days when our husbands are physically by our sides. Jonathan Swift put it simply: "May you live all the days of your life."[1] If we spent each deployment on the sidelines, waiting to enjoy life again until he came home, not only would that be an unfulfilling existence for us, but just imagine how much pressure that would put on our husbands to make us happy!

Psalm 28:7 says, "The Lord is my strength and my shield; my heart trusts in him, and I am helped. My heart leaps for joy and I will give thanks to him in song."

Our husbands do bring us joy, but our happiness is not up to them. If we're going to have joy, we simply must put our trust in the One who never changes, never leaves us, and never disappoints: Jesus. "I have come that they may have life, and have it to the full" (John 10:10). Through Him, we will have the full measure of joy within us (John 17:13), instead of feeling half-empty when our "other half" is gone.

We may be counting the days until an R&R or a homecoming, but I am convinced that God wants us to experience joy between those events, as well.

Navy wife Denise McColl contributed to the first *Faith Deployed*, but before the book was published, and mere months after her husband retired, Denise lost her battle to cancer. *How tragic,* I thought, *that she died so soon after her husband came home to be with her for good!* But consider how *much more* tragic it would have been if Denise had forfeited her joy during deployments or until her husband's retirement. That would have been far, far worse. Instead, Denise experienced the joy of the Lord and was an active, joyful participant throughout her years.

Ask

Where can I find joy today?
Am I trusting God to fill me with joy, or my husband?

Pray

Lord, I praise You that I don't have to wait for the perfect circumstances to experience the full measure of Your joy. Help me to have a cheerful heart as I live all the days of my life. In Jesus' Name, Amen.

by Catherine Fitzgerald

Broken AND ALONE

He heals the brokenhearted and binds up their wounds.
PSALM 147:3

★ ★ ★

"DON'T GET YOUR HOPES UP," I said as my husband and I entered the doctor's office. It was our eight-week checkup on a pregnancy that came just two months after a miscarriage. I hadn't allowed myself to be excited, but my husband had already begun to rejoice. The nurse squeezed the cold gel onto my stomach and started searching for a sign of life. A furrow formed in her brow as she tilted her head.

"I'm going to get the doctor." *Oh God, please not again*. The doctor came in and searched again.

"I'm sorry," he said. I didn't hear much past that.

In the car as I sobbed inconsolably, my husband stared blankly ahead.

Within weeks, my husband deployed and I was left picking up the pieces of my broken heart alone. Military life doesn't stop for our personal tragedies. While at first I thought deployment was another disappointment, I began to see the blessing that God provided.

My heart needed some intensive care. The wounds were gushing, and He needed to bind them tightly. Unfortunately, I have a tendency to give God my watered-down complaints and cries because I first express them to my husband before bringing them to Him. This time, the healing power of my Father alone would be my only salve.

It's easy in the wake of a tragedy to view deployment as another blow to our already breathless gut. Yet often, it is just what the doctor ordered. The aloneness afforded to us by our spouse's absence is the opportunity for God to get deep into our wounds and bring about healing. He is "close to the brokenhearted and saves those who are crushed in spirit" (Psalm 34:18). Sometimes we are unaware of that rescue when our husband is home because our natural tendency is to turn to our earthly bridegroom first.

Hannah understood the bitterness that accompanies an empty womb. Unable to get pregnant, she knew that the only one that could handle this kind of pain was her God. "In her deep anguish Hannah prayed to the Lord, weeping bitterly" (1 Samuel 1:10). After she poured out her brokenness before her King "her face was no longer downcast" (1 Samuel 1:18).

If catastrophe strikes before deployment, allow God to use the quietness of a separation from your spouse for Him to draw nearer to you. Let His Word be the ointment to your brokenness. In His sovereignty, He has planned for you a season of restoration with Him and Him alone.

Ask

How can a separation become my season of restoration?
What brokenness do I need to bring before God
while my husband is away?

Pray

Father, in the midst of this storm, I need You to draw close to me. Without the companionship of the man You have given me, I desire Your salvation alone. Help me to lift my hands to praise You for this season of healing. In Jesus' Name, Amen.

by Alane Pearce

BUYING *Coffee*

In my distress I called to the Lord; I cried to my God for help, From his temple he heard my voice; my cry came before him, into his ears.
PSALM 18:6

WE HAD JUST TEN DAYS' NOTICE for my husband's deployment—only three months after he returned from eight months in Al Dhafra. While I canceled vacation plans and got him packed, my husband attended his appointments and got powers of attorney. His departure date quickly approached. We were both running on adrenaline and had little time to process what was going on.

A week after he left, I woke up crying and could not stop. Every time I opened my mouth—and sometimes when I didn't—I was overcome by a hurricane of weeping and sobbing. I was worried; I never reacted to anything with such force, and now I was wondering if I'd be able to make it through the day.

Four days later, I was still crying. I curled up in a chair and bawled. With gasps of air I begged God for an answer. All I heard was, "Call the doctor." So I did. And when they told me that they could see me in three weeks, the waterworks started again.

Long story short, I ended up seeing a counselor to help sort out my emotions, and I learned something very important from her about self-care. I complained one day about how I hated cleaning out the coffee pot. It was another thing I had to do myself and I was tired of it. "So buy your coffee from a coffee shop until you can handle cleaning out the pot," she said. It was so simple! Her advice gave me some relief.

I also found relief through the words of the Psalms—many of them were written out of fear and distress and their words ring true.

When you are unable to handle something, whether it's big or small, God wants you to give it to Him. He'll hear you when you call, and He'll tell you what to do. Then take appropriate action.

Tired of cleaning the house? Hire help for a month or two to give yourself a break. Need relief from the stresses of parenting by yourself? Get a sitter. Is the house a mess? Leave it for a bit or hire help. Weary of doing dishes? Use paper plates and throw them away! Sick of cooking? Cereal works!

Part of self-care is remembering that when you are in a deployed family, you can't do it all. You have to relax your standards and give yourself a break. Cast your cares on the Lord; He will hear you and show you where you can rest. That's a promise.

Ask

What is too hard for me right now?
Is there something I can "hire out" until I feel better?
What does God say about it?

Pray

God, I am overwhelmed. I am anxious (worried, concerned) about ______________ and I need relief. I put this problem in Your capable hands and I ask that You will show me how to deal with it. Let me feel Your peace as You show me how to take care of myself right now. In Jesus' Name, Amen.

by Angela Caban

THE GOD WHO SEES *Me*

Turn to me and be gracious to me,
for I am lonely and afflicted.
PSALM 25:16

WHEN MY HUSBAND DEPLOYED for the first time with the Army National Guard, it wasn't long before I started to feel abandoned, lonely, and anguished. The nearest base was forty minutes away and my husband's unit did not offer much support for the families.

Loneliness consumed my daily life like a dark shadow. I needed military friends, support, and guidance. I wanted someone to give me advice, speak to me from experience, and tell me they knew what I was feeling. Instead, I felt as though I was shunned from the Active community because my husband was Guard, and the Guard community rarely had any events or support groups available to us. I felt like I was invisible and insignificant.

But God didn't see me that way.

In the Old Testament, Sarai sent her handmaiden, Hagar, to Abram's bed to conceive a child on Sarai's behalf. When Hagar became pregnant, Sarai's jealousy turned to rage and the pregnant slave girl fled to the wilderness.

But it was there that the Angel of God met Hagar and called her *by name* (Genesis 16:8). After they spoke, Hagar *gave* God a name: *El Roi,* "the God who sees me" (Genesis 16:13).

Hagar the slave girl, unwanted and unloved by everyone around her, was the only person in the Bible to ever give God a name! *El Roi* expressed the comforting theological truth that she was not invisible to God. Carolyn Custis James says this:

In her encounter with the Angel of God, Hagar received dignity and meaning. The simple but unchanging truth that God's eyes were fixed on her empowered her with a kind of freedom no one could ever take away. She was not alone. She *did* matter. This freed her to do the extraordinary—to love her neighbor . . . and to reflect the image of God in her relationships.[2]

God saw Hagar, and He sees me too, when no one else seems to notice. Whether you are a Guard, Reserve, or Active duty wife yourself, I'm sure you have also experienced intense loneliness and isolation. God is the God who sees you too. We are not invisible to Him. And in our loneliness, God pulls us close.

When we are assured of God's love for us, we, like Hagar, are more able to love our neighbors, too. I asked for God's help, and He guided me to reach out and form a support group on Facebook. Within the next few weeks I started to feel peace with my husband's deployment and I no longer felt lonely. I had the support of my family, new friends, and most importantly, God.

Ask

Am I handing over my worries to the Lord?
Am I overcome with the fear of being lonely that
I am not trusting in the Lord?

Pray

Lord, I turn to You as my source of strength when I am feeling so alone. Thank You for being so accessible and understanding. Help me to overcome my isolation and to reach out to others once again. In Jesus' Name, Amen.

by April Lakata Cao

Bridging THE PARENTING GAP

A father to the fatherless, a defender of widows,
is God in his holy dwelling.
PSALM 68:5

★ ★ ★

AS THE WIFE of an active duty service member it was inevitable that I would find myself parenting without my husband. Between training and deployments I learned to walk the tightrope of a single parent and reconciled myself to being both mother and father to our two children. My son Gabriel made it quite clear, however, that the influence of his father could not be duplicated. He was angry and resentful, pushing back at every turn despite my best efforts. I wept with the enormity of the loss they both felt in his absence and began to pray for God to bridge the gap of my inadequacies.

In time I realized that military wives don't have to be a dad to our children but can trust in God's character as our perfect Father. "I will be a Father to you, and you will be my sons and daughters, says the Lord Almighty" (2 Corinthians 6:18). When we surrender our children's hearts to their heavenly Father and invite Him into a partnership with us in parenting, the burden of guilt that comes with our imperfections is greatly eased.

Parenting without the daily feedback and input from our helpmate creates unique challenges—especially in the area of discipline. Remember, however, when we partner with the Lord we are asking Him to take an active role in the discipline process and guide us down a path that will not only resolve conflict but exemplify God's unconditional love. "No discipline seems pleasant at the time, but painful. Later on, however, it produces a harvest of righteousness and peace for those who have been trained by it" (Hebrews 12:11). Loving correction is necessary to help children develop the whole character of God. Discipline, as loving correction, is a process of teaching and training within the confines of a godly home.

We can also rest in the assurance that as our Father, God is a steadfast Counselor, Advocate, and Comforter during the parenting process. "But the Counselor, the Holy Spirit, whom the Father will send in my name, will teach you all things and will remind you of everything I have said to you. Peace I leave with you; my peace I give you" (John 14:26–27).

What a blessing we have in the Holy Spirit who stands ready to offer us direction, advice, and mediation as we confront daily obstacles. In turn we can prayerfully pass along His comfort and peace to our children and guide them in their decisions while encouraging their own spiritual growth.

Ask

Will I trust God completely with the hearts of my children?
Are we relying on God's character as the
foundation of our parenting?

Pray

Lord, I know that I cannot be everything that my children need but what I can do is invite You to be in partnership with me in all circumstances. Please help me bridge the gap, to stand in the place of my inadequacies so that I may lead according to Your will. Thank You for the blessing of my family, and may they learn to seek You through my example. In Jesus' Name. Amen.

by Bettina Dowell

Unexpected

For you are with me.
PSALM 23:4B

★ ★ ★

MY HUSBAND HAD PATIENTLY listened while I talked late one night, then changed not only our discussion, but our lives, with his announcement: "When I went to reserves today, there were four hundred day orders to Iraq lying on my desk." Ironically, he had gone into reserves planning to work on his retirement papers, as he was scheduled to retire in just five months.

So what is a woman of faith to do when her life takes an unexpected, not especially positive, turn? God graciously gave me answers from His Word as I tried to absorb my husband's announcement. He laid counsel out for me in the form of a funny little acronym (acronyms always speak to this military wife's heart): FRBLO

Footprints—"Show me your ways, O Lord, teach me your paths" (Psalms 25:4). God had challenged me that year to focus on decreasing my carbon footprint and increasing my spiritual footprint. As we allow our feet to follow in His path, we are able to walk the journey before us.

Rest—"Find rest, O my soul, in God alone; my hope comes from Him." (Psalm 62:5). When the unexpected appears, my first reaction is to "fix" the situation. God encourages us to rest and trust Him instead.

Beg—"Trust in him at all times, O people; pour out your

hearts to him, for God is our refuge" (Psalm 62:8). We are told to beg for God's assistance, pouring out our questions, fears, and frustrations before Him. We need to be desperate for God and rely on His strength.

Listen—"Pray continually" (1 Thessalonians 5:17). Praying and reading the Bible keeps us listening and focused on what God has to say about the "unexpecteds" in our lives.

Obey—"To obey is better than sacrifice" (1 Samuel 15:22b). Though deployments present many unknowns, it our job to do the things God has already shown us, through His Word, He wants us to do. Obedience is key.

In her book *Tour of Duty*, Sara Horn calls the unexpected turns "detours" and reminds us that "detours are not roadblocks. What we see as obstacles, God may choose to use as a bridge to bring us closer to where He wants us. Detours often help transition us from one phase of life to another. They move us from where we stand to where we belong."[3]

FRBLO—five little letters God used to fill my heart with His peace in this unexpected place in my life. He is waiting to do the same for you.

Ask

Where is God asking you to trust Him in
something unexpected in your life?
Will you ask Him to help you to follow Him, rest in Him,
beg Him, listen to Him, and obey Him?

Pray

Father, please help me trust You when my life takes unexpected turns. Help me find peace by following You, resting in You, begging You, listening to You, and obeying You. In Jesus' Name, Amen.

by Alane Pearce

LITTLE *Indiscretions*

As obedient children, do not conform to the evil desires you had when you lived in ignorance. But just as he who called you is holy, so be holy in all you do.
1 PETER 1:14–15

ALL THAT MONEY coming in when my husband was deployed was seductive. We decided together to pay off our bills so we could live debt free, but there was this program that I wanted to try because I needed to lose weight and it wasn't cheap. I thought to myself, "I'll just cut back elsewhere and do it." I didn't even consult him. It seemed like such a little thing—but it was out of character for me. We usually made all of our buying decisions together.

That little indiscretion led to others; telling white lies, making unbudgeted purchases, avoiding questions about how the bills were coming along. I found myself caught in a big web of deceitfulness that led me away from the holiness I was called to as a follower of Jesus.

It is easy to be lured into the grey areas of right and wrong, especially when your husband is so far away and unable to immediately see or comment on your decisions. It's simple to not mention something on the phone or avoid answering a question in an e-mail. It's easier to hide indiscretions like flirting with an office mate or confiding in a man other than your husband when your spouse is gone. But this is when it is even more important to be obedient and not conforming to the evil desires of the world because things can easily go too far.

Holiness means that we are set apart and should act differently than those around us. It means we do not give in to temptation because we hold ourselves accountable to the One who sees everything: God alone.

So what do you do when you feel tempted to do something you shouldn't? First, remember that you are called by Christ to be holy in all you do. Always.

Next, take every thought captive and make it obedient to Christ (2 Corinthians 10:5). There is a song warning that a little thought or a second glance can easily lure us to wanting more of what we shouldn't have; in other words, "Be careful, little eyes, what you see." Take each thought that pops into your mind and compare it to God's will for your life. If it doesn't conform to holiness, kick it out!

Finally, avoid temptations all together. Second Corinthians 7:1 says, "Let us purify ourselves from everything that contaminates body and spirit, perfecting holiness out of reverence for God." It is much better to run from temptation than to entertain it.

Remember, you are called to holiness, and God gives you the ability to strive toward it.

Ask

Is my mind dwelling on things I shouldn't have or do,
or am I taking each thought captive?
Are all my actions representing my holiness?

Pray

Father, please make me aware of unholy thoughts or desires in my mind and heart. Help me take each thought captive and make it obedient to Christ. Purify me from everything that contaminates my body and spirit to perfect my holiness out of reverence to You. In Jesus' Name, Amen.

by Bettina Dowell

THE ABSENT *Leader*

For the husband is the head of the wife as Christ is the head of the church, His body, of which He is the Savior.
EPHESIANS 5:23

IT WAS THANKSGIVING, but the husband and dad of our family would not be sitting at the head of the table this particular year. We were missing him and looking for a way to let him feel included in our celebration. We wanted to reassure each other that we were still a family, though one that was stretched across thousands of miles.

My daughter made a pecan pie and shipped it to Iraq. We scheduled our dinnertime to coincide with a time Rob could Skype with us. When it was time to eat, we opened up the laptop and sat our husband and father at the head of the table. He said the blessing and thanked God for the fact that we were able to share time together through the gift of technology, reminding all of us that ultimately God was our Leader and Provider, even when we were apart. While we laughed and enjoyed our dinner, Rob joined us at dessert with a piece of pecan pie. Throughout the deployment, the memories of that day served as beautiful reminders that we were still a family, and my husband had been given the assignment from God to sit at the head of our family.

Moses and Aaron provide us an example from the Bible of what can happen if we ignore the priorities of our absent leaders. After the Israelites had been released from slavery in Egypt, they stopped to camp while Moses went up the mountain to receive instructions from God. While Moses was absent, the people asked Aaron, whom Moses had left in charge, to make new gods for them.

Rather than saying no to the people and reminding them of the commission he and Moses had been given to lead them under God's direction, Aaron chose to please the voices of those in closest proximity. When Moses came down and saw the Israelites worshipping a golden calf idol that Aaron had fashioned, he confronted Aaron. "Moses saw that the people were running wild and that Aaron had let them get out of control and so become a laughingstock to their enemies" (Exodus 32:25).

Certainly, there are days when we feel like we have let those under our charge "run wild" and "get out of control" while spouses are deployed. However, we need to continue to refocus our families back on the priorities of our absent leaders while they are away. Even the small gestures, like a Skype call, a prayer, or a piece of pie can go a long way in reminding us who God has given the responsibility of being the leader of our home to and how we can honor their priorities.

How can I reinforce my husband's role as the
leader of our home while he is away?
What would mean the most to my children and me
in our particular season of life?

Dear Lord, thank You for setting up order in our homes and families. Help me not to be discouraged by my spouse's absence, but be creative in supporting him as the leader of our home. In Jesus' Name, Amen.

by Catherine Fitzgerald

Change IS GOOD

There is a time for everything, and a season for every activity under the heavens.
ECCLESIASTES 3:1

ONE OF THE GREATEST blessings I have found in this military life is the exact thing that most wives find to be the biggest curse: time apart. Before you go thinking what an awful wife I am, let me explain. When my husband is gone, I get a unique opportunity that most married women do not have. After my duties are done each day, I have time. Time to read books I've always wanted to read. Time to explore my inner thoughts that can often get pushed to the back burner. Time to try new recipes that my "meat and potatoes" man might not be so keen about. Time to spend more of my day in God's Word and in conversation with Him. While I undeniably would much rather have the love of my life by my side, I have learned to embrace this very special gift of time given to us as military wives.

Paul knew that those of us who marry would face a pull in our lives. "An unmarried woman . . . is concerned about the Lord's affairs: Her aim is to be devoted to the Lord in both body and spirit. But a married woman is concerned about the affairs of this world—how she can please her husband" (1 Corinthians 7:34). We certainly still feel that tug when our husband is gone, but that physical absence can turn our focus from our earthly bridegroom to our heavenly one. It can also focus us on the interests we may have had before we got married or even newly discovered ones. We can grow leaps and bounds in our spiritual, physical, and mental selves if we use the gift of time wisely.

In fact, sometimes we can grow so much that when our husband returns, there can be friction as we try to settle back into a marriage with a new, improved version of the woman he left behind and a man who has been altered by his own experiences. Sometimes the changes that occur during a deployment go unseen on the surface and can lead to an inexplicable source of conflict. When you miss the incremental day-to-day changes in someone else's life, a reunion can be riddled with bumps and bruises as you each try to get to know each other again. There are plenty of practical ways you can protect your relationship from that difficult terrain:

1. Keep a journal and share them with each other.
2. Find new hobbies you can do together and grow in a *new* way, jointly.
3. Take the time to reconnect after a deployment. Discuss the ways you have grown and what changes you want to make in your life.

Ask

Am I using our time apart to grow myself spiritually as well as in other areas?
How can I share the ways I am changing with my husband and vice versa?

Pray

Father, allow this separation be a time for both my husband and me to grow as individuals. Use this distance to mature us in You. Help us to reconnect as two changed people, coming back together as one flesh. In Jesus' Name, Amen.

by Rosie Williams

WATCHES OF THE *Night*

Arise, cry out in the night, as the watches of the night begin; pour out your heart like water in the presence of the Lord.
LAMENTATIONS 2:19

★ ★ ★

ALTHOUGH FATIGUE can be overwhelming, not being able to fall asleep is a common problem. If deployment is involved, the result is often a gut-wrenching fear that stops sleep dead in its tracks. The problems of the day are often magnified as night descends.

Years ago, when my husband was in Vietnam, I was terrified that he would not come home. One fearful thought after another tumbled into my mind as I tossed and turned trying to find peaceful rest. One sleepless night, I got up and opened my Bible to Psalm 91:5–7: "You will not fear the terror of night, nor the arrow that flies by day, nor the pestilence that stalks in the darkness, nor the plague that destroys at midday. A thousand may fall at your side, ten thousand at your right hand, but it will not come near you." Years later, I realized that over the centuries, this psalm has been known as the Soldier's Prayer (or Psalm), but that night it was new to me and a personal affirmation that God was with me and my husband.

In Psalm 6, David finds himself faint-hearted, ill, and anguished within. David was overcome with attacks from his enemies, and all night long he was worn out, but couldn't sleep because of his sorrow and weeping. He cried out to God in prayer. Psalm 6:8–9 says, "Away from me, all you who do evil, for the Lord has heard my weeping. The Lord has heard my cry for mercy; the Lord accepts my prayer."

You too can be assured that God will hear your cry for help. If you find yourself in the middle of a long sleepless night, it may be a "wake up call" or an opportunity to pour out your heart to Him about the things that are troubling you. Once you have experienced reading a special verse of reassurance or having a quiet time of prayer, perhaps the next time you can't sleep, you may even have a keen sense of anticipation as you approach this uninterrupted time with God.

Psalm 94:19 says, "When anxiety was great within me, your consolation brought joy to my soul." God has a consolation, or word of comfort, for each anxious thought that threatens to steal your sleep. "When you lie down, you will not be afraid; when you lie down, your sleep will be sweet. Have no fear of sudden disaster or of the ruin that overtakes the wicked, for the Lord will be your confidence and will keep your foot from being snared" (Proverbs 3:24–26).

Ask

Are you experiencing anxious thoughts that make it difficult to sleep?
Can you think of times in your past where God has provided comfort that has relieved your mind?

Pray

Dear Lord, You have promised that I can cast my care upon You, because You care for me. Please give me a sense of Your presence with me as I pour out my heart to You today. Help me to find rest in You. In Jesus' Name, Amen.

by Bettina and Libby Dowell

Gimmes FOR TEENS

He reveals deep and hidden things.
DANIEL 2:22A

★ ★ ★

AS MOTHER AND DAUGHTER, the upcoming deployment was uncharted territory for us. Never had we been at home without any of our men. But as the two older brothers moved to California and our husband/dad left for Iraq, we were suddenly left with a chick house for the first time in either of our lives.

The next months were a journey where God taught us many things, some that were deep and hidden, about ourselves, our relationship, and each other. Having a parent deployed during the tumultuous tide of the teen years provides unique challenges, as does the parenting of those teens. The "gimmes" are some of the lessons God taught us about what teens need during deployment, as told through a teenager's voice.

Gimme Freedom: Though I don't understand what it is like to be married, I have lived in your home long enough to know having your best friend away is no fun for you. Please, however, do not ask me to consistently take their place as your companion. I want to be able to go and hang out with my friends without feeling I am deserting you. "But there is a friend who sticks closer than a brother" (Proverbs 18:24b).

Gimme Responsibility: Trust me, I will probably never ask for this, but I need it. Let me empty the dishwasher, put away the groceries, or put up the Christmas lights. It does not help me to watch you exhaust yourself trying to do it all alone. "Lazy hands make for poverty, but diligent hands bring wealth" (Proverbs 10:4).

Gimme Celebrations: Though you may feel like the last thing you want to do this year is put up a Christmas tree, please don't ask that our lives stop because someone is gone. I still need to celebrate, laugh, and enjoy our family traditions—even if they have to be modified. Seeing you laugh too makes me feel better. "You turned my wailing into dancing; you removed my sackcloth and clothed me with joy" (Psalm 30:11).

Gimme Space: And last, but most importantly, please understand that this is a roller coaster for both of us. Whether I am sullen, withdrawn, acting unaffected, or just plain grouchy, please understand this is not an easy road for me either. I don't have all the answers, but please allow me some space to establish my relationship with my deployed parent in ways that work for me. I may not do it like you would, but sometimes I really do know what it will take to get me through this season (unless my behavior becomes destructive to myself or others). Thank you for understanding that everyone handles things differently. "Those who guard their mouths and their tongues keep themselves from calamity" (Proverbs 21:23).

Ask

In what ways could I give my teen freedom, responsibility, celebration, and space?
In what areas do I need to listen more and talk less?

Pray

Dear Lord, help me to understand that deployment is as disconcerting for my teens as it is for me. Please help me to give them the things they need to draw closer to You, and to my spouse and me, during this season. In Jesus' Name, Amen.

by Jill Bozeman with Jocelyn Green

DADDY'S *Presence*

Let us fix our eyes on Jesus, the author
and perfecter of our faith.
HEBREWS 12:2

DURING ONE PARTICULAR deployment, I spoke to my daughter's school counselor about how the children were coping with their dad's absence. "The kids know exactly how many birthdays Dad has missed, and it really affects them," she told me. But when I asked my daughter about it later, she looked at me strangely and shrugged her shoulders. "Mom," she said, "I have no idea!"

My daughter could tell me when she remembered him there, but couldn't say for sure that he was NOT there from one time to the next. Because you see, Daddy was part of our everyday life; even when he was absent, he was with us.

She remembers the flowers he sent on her last day of school during a deployment to Afghanistan, and the Hello Kitty Alarm clock that came in the mail when he was stationed in Korea. She remembers the cards, and letters, and the DVDs of Daddy reading books. She remembers the telephone calls and the pictures all over the house. She remembers the planning and anticipating and the talk about Daddy's homecoming. Her daddy was in her heart every single day.

Since the moment Jesus ascended to heaven, and sat down at the right hand of the Father, we could say that He has missed well over two thousand birthdays. Yet, He promises He is always with us, and we continually focus on what is eternal (2 Corinthians 4:17–18)!

Two families can go through the exact same deployment cycle, or even a similar military life journey, but because of where they place their focus, they will have entirely different experiences. The choice is ours. The stakes are high—the minds, hearts, and attitudes of our families. We can either live our military lives victoriously, confident in the goodness and sovereignty of God, or in defeat, as victims of circumstances beyond our control.

Joyce Meyer says, "If you are going to win the battle of the mind and defeat your enemy, where you focus your attention is crucial. The more you meditate on God's Word, the stronger you'll become and the more easily you'll win the victories."[4]

Meditating on God's Word means thinking about it seriously, talking about it, and letting it affect our lives. My daughter didn't just *notice* her daddy's phone calls, letters, and gifts. She took them to heart so much that she felt his presence even when he did, in fact, miss her birthday. If we take to heart God's own letter to us (His Word), we will know His presence much more, as well. When we fix our eyes on Jesus, all other concerns fade to the background.

Ask

What am I spending most of my energy focusing on?
How can I spend more time meditating on God's Word?

Pray

Dear Lord, forgive me for giving place to the enemy by focusing on what things are not. Instead, fill my heart with Your vision and Your purpose for tomorrow. Create in me a grateful heart filled with thanksgiving! And keep my eyes fixed on the prize, with praise in my mouth! In Jesus' Name, Amen.

by Sarah Ball

NEVER-ENDING DAYS, EVERLASTING *God*

Do you not know? Have you not heard? The Lord is the everlasting God, the Creator of the ends of the earth. He will not grow tired or weary, and his understanding no one can fathom. He gives strength to the weary and increases the power of the weak.

ISAIAH 40:28–29

★ ★ ★

ALL I REALLY WANTED was a smoothie. It was month #10 of deployment, and I'd had a brutal week.

My daughter came home from school with her expensive glasses in hand—snapped in half. Our garage door had malfunctioned again, twisting into a semi-closed position that screamed "Big repair bill!" to everyone who drove by.

I was heading my children toward bed when my daughter called, "Mom! Come take a look at the carpet!" The handiwork of my one-year-old on the carpet required shampooing—immediately. Scrubbing the carpet, I told myself, "Just finish this job, and the day will be done. Just get through this, make a delicious smoothie, and the day will be redeemed."

With the carpet finished, I set up my blender, dumped in the fruit and yogurt, and hit the button. The blender buzzed for a moment, then blew out. I won't describe my reaction in detail, but it wasn't pretty. I was exhausted, I was emotionally depleted, and I *really* wanted a smoothie.

A friend once told me that her biggest battle was against

weariness—she felt like she never regained her strength before it was time for the next deployment. Our daily fatigue can begin to accumulate until we feel completely weary.

Thankfully, we have the words of Isaiah to put our weariness in perspective. Yes, we become tired at the end of each day, but we serve an everlasting God who does not become tired or weary, no matter how long the deployment lasts. When we begin to understand the eternal nature of our God, our tiring days become much smaller by comparison.

God's chosen nation of Israel certainly understood tiring days. They spent forty years wandering in a desert while God prepared them to enter their Promised Land, and God met all of their needs. They ate manna every sunrise and meat at dusk. Their shoes and clothes never wore out (Deuteronomy 29:5). God will meet your needs too.

Are you feeling weary from never-ending days on this journey through military life? Read the verses of Isaiah 40:28–29 again. Take hope in the Lord; wait for new strength from Him. You walk with the Everlasting God, who delights in giving strength to the weary and power to the weak.

Ask

Am I relying on my own strength to finish each day or am I seeking strength from God?
Do I trust the Everlasting God to bring me through the challenges I will face today?

Pray

Dear Lord, I praise You for being the Everlasting God who does not become weary or tired. I bring You my weariness, asking that You lift its weight from me. Please give me Your strength, so I may walk through this day and not become weary. In Jesus' Name, Amen.

by Bettina Dowell

Held UP

When Moses' hands grew tired, they took a stone and put it under him and he sat on it. Aaron and Hur held his hands up—one on one side, one on the other—so that his hands remained steady till sunset.
EXODUS 17:12

AS A YOUNG MARINE WIFE with a husband deployed in a combat zone, Corinne Shuster knew she needed support. She had been blessed to be surrounded by many supportive family members and friends. What frustrated her was that she felt she was drawing all of her support from those friends and family, not from God.

Corinne describes something she learned during that deployment, early in her husband's military career: "A very special friend pointed something out to me I hadn't thought about before. By leaning on the members of Christ's church, I was in fact leaning on Him—because the church is the Body of Christ . . . Because of [the church], I see and feel Him all around me, all the time. "[5]

Corinne's struggle was not unlike the struggle Moses faced during the Israelites battle with the Amalekites told in the book of Exodus, chapter 17. As the Israelites fought, Moses raised his hands toward heaven during the battle. As long as Moses's hands stayed in the air, the Israelites were winning. When Moses lowered his hands, Israel began to lose the battle.

The problem for Moses was that he became too tired to lift his hands alone any longer. So Aaron and Hur came beside him and held his hands in the air. With support from others, Moses's hands remained in the air until Israel won the battle.

How often, as military wives, do we feel we can no longer go forward in our daily battles? We want to trust God with all of our struggles, but physically we have run out of gas for whatever we may be facing. Like Corinne, we can be blessed when we realize that dependence on the body of Christ to hold us up when we are struggling is sometimes exactly what God desires from us. The humility required in allowing others to serve us can be difficult, but so important in our journey of faith. When we allow the body of Christ to support us, we bless others by letting them use the gifts and strengths God has given them to share in His work. Just like Aaron and Hur assisted Moses in leading the Israelites to victory in battle, when we allow others to hold us up, we allow them to be a part of the victory God desires for all of us.

In what areas can I allow others to hold me up during the daily battles of military life? In what areas do I need to exercise humility in order for others to take part in the victory God wants to bring about in my life?

Dear Father, some days the challenges of being a military spouse feel like battles in my life. Please help me to humbly accept support from those who desire to hold me up in the fight. In Jesus' Name, Amen.

Section Four

SOUL ARMOR:

Guarding against Spiritual Attacks

For our struggle is not against flesh and blood,
but against the rulers, against the authorities, against the
powers of this dark world and against the spiritual
forces of evil in the heavenly realms.

EPHESIANS 6:11

by Rosie Williams

THE ARMOR OF *Light*

The night is nearly over, the day is almost here. So let us put aside the deeds of darkness, and put on the armor of light. Clothe yourselves with the Lord Jesus Christ and do not think about how to gratify the desires of the sinful nature.
ROMANS 13:12, 14

THE BIBLE GIVES SEVERAL analogies regarding our spiritual "dress." A passage in Ephesians 6:10–19 tells us to put on the full armor of God, which at times has been hard for me to relate to. How is it that a woman can put on the armor of God in order to be dressed and ready for service (Luke 12:35)?

As I looked closer at Ephesians 6 through a "pink lens," I noticed that the overall purpose of the armor is protection. It is in the heart of a woman to want and need an umbrella of protection from the harshness of the world. The Bible tells us how to protect ourselves from the harshness of Satan himself.

Since each piece of the armor is a name of God, we are putting on Christ himself. When we are "dressed and ready," others can see Christ when they look at us. Consider the following:

Truth: As we put on truth, we can be set free to be the woman God designed us to be. The truth is that Jesus is the way we can come into the presence of our heavenly Father (John 14:6).

Righteousness: The breastplate of righteousness protects the heart from assaults from the enemy. Only in Christ can we live a righteous life. Jeremiah 23:6 says one of God's names is "The Lord Our Righteousness."

Peace: Jesus is the One who can calm our anxious heart. To shod our feet with the preparation of the gospel of peace refers to a believer's stability or sure-footedness, which allows us to stand firm in the battle. "For he himself is our peace" (Ephesians 2:14).

Faith: The shield of faith is important to protect us from the enemy. A Christian's resolute faith in the Lord can stop and extinguish all the flaming arrows of the evil one aimed at us. "He is the faithful God" (Deuteronomy 7:9).

Salvation: Helmet of salvation implies protecting your head, mind, heart, and very identity. By personally accepting God's gift of salvation, we rest assured that we will live eternally with Christ in heaven. "He is my rock and my salvation" (Psalm 62:6).

Word of God: As we hide God's Word, the Bible, in our hearts, we develop a close personal relationship with our Savior. The Sword of the Spirit is the only offensive weapon; it is powerful for discerning God's will and is a baseline for our beliefs (Hebrews 4:12).

Prayer: Prayer keeps us alert as we ask the Lord to clothe us with the armor, with himself, and with the light of Christ. We are to "always pray and not give up" (Luke 18:1).

Ask

What are some practical ways you can put on God's armor?
Why do we need a spiritual armor?

Pray

Dear Lord, thank You for the protection offered through Your Word. Show me how to be a woman warrior. Be my strength and armor of light in this dark world. In Jesus' Name, Amen.

by Jocelyn Green

TACTICS

For our struggle is not against flesh and blood,
but against . . . the powers of this dark world and against
the spiritual forces of evil in the heavenly realms.
EPHESIANS 6:12

WHILE OUR DEPLOYED service members fight in the combat zone, the battle on the home front takes place in our minds and spirits. Our enemy has no face, but many names: anger, bitterness, discouragement, insecurity, jealousy, despair. We must be alert to Satan's tactics. The following are just a few of them.

1. **He tempts us with what seems attractive but ultimately harms us.** That forbidden piece of fruit sure looked good to Eve. Nothing about the fruit itself had any hint of harm about it, making it easy for Satan to tempt her with it. We all know the rest of the story.

I know of a military wife who carpooled with her neighbor to choir practice while her husband was deployed. It seemed practical, but one thing led to another and the two ended up having an affair.

2. **He plants doubt about or contradicts God's Word.** In Genesis 3:1, Satan questioned what God said. Next, he blatantly told Eve God had lied to her (Genesis 3:4). He wants us to doubt the Scriptures too. *God isn't really good after all. God isn't listening to you.* Any time you hear little whispers of decep-

tion like this, don't trust your feelings, but trust your Bible!

3. **He tries to twist Scripture for his purposes.** In Luke 4:9–10, Satan quotes Scripture to Jesus, misusing Psalm 91:11–12. If Satan can get us to claim only half a verse, such as "I can do all things" without "through him who strengthens me" (Philippians 4:13 ESV), he will have accomplished his purpose as well. We must be vigilant about understanding God's Word in its proper context.

4. **He comes at us when we are most vulnerable and alone.** Both Eve and Jesus were alone when Satan tempted them. Military wives, be on your guard against the enemy, especially when you are alone. Think about other times you're vulnerable. Maybe it's when you're tired or if you haven't been to church in a while. These are Satan's "opportune times" (Luke 4:13).

5. **He even uses well-meaning Christians who have good motives.** In Matthew 16:21–23, Peter rebukes Jesus for predicting his own death—and Jesus calls him "Satan"! I imagine Peter was shocked to his core; but his words refuted God's will. Not only do we need to weigh what our friends say against Scripture, we need to be careful that we are not that well-meaning person Satan uses to give false counsel, as well.

Ask

What makes me most vulnerable to Satan's tactics?
How can I guard against those times?
Which tactics have I seen him try on me already?

Pray

Lord, help me be strong in Your power and put on the armor of God so I can resist Satan's schemes. When I stumble, forgive me, and help me stand up again in Your strength. In Jesus' Name, Amen.

by Patti Katter

DO NOT *Fear*

For I am the Lord, your God, who takes hold of your right hand and says to you, Do not fear; I will help you.
ISAIAH 41:13

WHETHER I WOULD TURN ON the TV for just a moment, or turn the computer on to check my e-mail, depressing headlines about our troops who were killed in Iraq assaulted me—and my husband was there in the midst of it all. Almost on a daily basis during a certain point in my husband's deployment, wives and families were informed of fatalities and casualties coming from my husband's unit.

I was afraid. Afraid that my husband would not come home from the war. Afraid of the uncertainties and possibilities. Afraid my children would no longer have a father. I didn't want my family or my friends to know I was afraid. After all, I was a military wife, strong and fearless to all looking in. I suppose most wives are afraid of the unknown at one time or another while their husbands are deployed. I believe that fear is an unspoken sketch that's drawn in the emotions of many military wives.

Fear can rule our lives if we allow it. It's very important to remember that the Lord has a plan for our life, and to trust God with our future.

My good friend Lorie, who lost her son in Iraq, constantly claims the verse Luke 12:7a: "Indeed, the very hairs of your head are all numbered." This verse has also helped me to remember that if the Lord knows the number of hairs on my head, surely He knows everything else about my life and the best thing is, He takes time to care.

Isaiah 41:10 says, "So do not fear, for I am with you; do not be dismayed, for I am your God. I will strengthen you and help you; I will uphold you with my righteous right hand."

True, God has not promised a trouble-free life for us. Christians suffer the loss of their loved ones every day. But God does promise to be with us through it all, carrying us through. Psalm 23:4 says, "Even though I walk through the valley of the shadow of death, I will fear no evil, for you are with me." Have you ever considered that in the valley of the shadow of death, Light is still present? It must be, or there would be no shadow, only darkness. God is with us no matter where we are (see also Joshua 1:9; Psalm 139:7–12).

When I was finally able to give all my concerns to God, including the safety of my husband, my relationship with God grew by leaps and bounds. I pray that you, too, can give everything over to the Lord, including the safety of your loved one.

What do I fear most, that I can release to the Lord?
Which Scripture verse can I memorize
to help soothe my fears?

Dear Lord and heavenly Father, I know You have a plan for my life. Please help me to put aside fears that distort my way of thinking. Fill my thoughts with thoughts of comfort and peace as I journey through deployment and this life. In Your precious Name I pray, Amen.

by Jocelyn Green

Voices

My sheep listen to my voice; I know them, and they follow me.
JOHN 10:27

"WHY CAN'T ROB DO IT? He's the husband. It's his job." The voice of my friend on the other end of the line crackled from five thousand miles away in righteous indignation, supposedly on my behalf. But on the inside, my spirit sank.

Before the phone call, it made perfect sense to me why Rob hadn't done whatever household chore was in question—he was at sea. I had the time. Still, the conversation unnerved me. Suddenly, I was tempted to take her side against him.

Voices are powerful. They can encourage and guide, or they can cast doubt on the blameless and justify sin. Often, the spirit behind what we hear can be traced back to Satan or to God. We must discern the difference.

Satan tries to discourage me with three recurring voices:

1. **The voice of accusation.** The example above falls under this category. Out of the blue, something I hear causes me to accuse someone of wrong. Instead of giving them the benefit of the doubt, I assume I know their heart's intention, when of course I don't (1 Samuel 16:7).

2. **The voice of exaggeration.** Exaggeration starts with a seed of truth—but it's still lying. Judy McChrystal, a veteran army wife of thirty-one years, reminds us, "We need to be more accurate about our feelings. This is hard, but I'm not

dying." Paul keeps exaggeration at bay in 2 Corinthians 4:8–9: "We are hard pressed on every side, but not crushed; perplexed, but not in despair; persecuted, but not abandoned; struck down, but not destroyed."

3. **The voice of condemnation.** When I sin, this voice riddles me with guilt, so I am almost paralyzed to do anything else. But God's Word gives us freedom: Jesus says to go and sin no more (John 8:11). "There is now no condemnation for those who are in Christ Jesus" (Romans 8:1).

These voices should not be heeded. But thankfully, God speaks to us, too. How will we know when it's Him?

Reread John 10:27. Lambs learn to recognize their shepherd's voice only by spending time with him. It's the same way for us. Priscilla Shirer says:

> Once we enter God's sheepfold and start to get to know him, intimacy builds. Eventually we come to know Him so well that we can know if He is speaking simply by asking, "Does this sound like God's voice?" . . . God's voice resonates within us because it speaks in a language that we, by the power of the Holy Spirit, can completely comprehend.[1]

Which voices seem to have the most influence
on my thoughts and actions?
Do those voices line up with Scripture, or not?

Lord, help me discern which voices are from the enemy. May I grow ever closer to You so that I recognize Your voice when You speak to me. In Jesus' Name, Amen.

by Rachel Latham

Nightmares

I will lie down and sleep in peace, for you alone,
O Lord, make me dwell in safety.
PSALM 4:8

I HAVE A RECURRING NIGHTMARE when my husband is deployed. In my dream, I am searching for my husband and children in a large building. I panic, moving from doorway to doorway searching for them, desperate to get everyone back together. Once, the building was filling with water and I was racing against time. Another time I was locked outside of the building. Not once did I ever succeed in finding my family. I always wake in a panic, unable to sleep.

After a night filled with nightmares, the morning is especially rough. Everything still needs to be done and the burdens of the day haven't disappeared. Only now, I need to do it in a mental fog, craving a night of rest without dreams.

During these times I have to step back and remember God's promises. My nightmares are a result of stress and worry and my desire that we be reunited as a family. It is not God's will for me to be so burdened that I cannot rest.

In the book of 1 Peter, Peter reminds us that our life is in God's care. In chapter 5, verse 7 we are told to cast our cares upon the Lord, because He cares for us. We also know through the book of James that the trying of our faith works patience. No one desires trials, but I do know that God will work it out for good. How I respond to trials will either build up my faith or tear it down.

When the nightmares come now, I spend my waking time memorizing Scriptures that contain God's promises of sleep, such as Psalm 4:8 above. I pray for my husband and my family and continue praying until I fall asleep. During the next day when I am tired, I try to eat healthy, energy building foods. I try to nap if possible. And when I am grumpy and overwhelmed, I let some other things slide and spend the time reading God's Word, praying and casting my cares. It is an active choice. If I didn't remember to do this, the day would be filled with angry outbursts and frustration. I have to remind myself to make a different choice and to draw close to God.

Are you burdened with the inability to sleep
while your husband is away?
Have you tried to allow this to grow your faith through
prayer and the casting of your cares upon the Lord?

Dear Lord, thank You for the promises in your Word. Your Word holds the answers that we need. Help me, Lord, to remember in the darkness of the night, to seek my comfort through You. Help me, Lord, to cast my concerns to You (and leave them there!), while I choose to rest in You. Thank You, Lord, that You are with us through the day and the night, and with our husbands wherever they may be. May my faith strengthen through this time. In Jesus' Name, Amen.

by Jocelyn Green

Freedom FROM SUSPICION

. . . [Love] always trusts, always hopes, always perseveres.
1 CORINTHIANS 13:7

ALMOST IMMEDIATELY AFTER Katherine Morris's deployed husband had an affair, he confessed and repented. But the damage to her trust was deep, and suspicion plagued her at every turn.

Even if there has never been an affair, insecurity is all too common among military wives who are separated from their husbands by time zones and oceans. *What is he doing over there? Who does he laugh with and confide in? Can he remain abstinent for several months on end?* If we are not careful, seeds of insecurity quickly grow into towering accusations of suspicion in the dark corners of our minds, whether or not they are justified.

I can't imagine the insecurity the wives in the Bible must have experienced. Just think of Rachel, who had been engaged to Jacob for seven years, then had to watch her father give her sister Leah to Jacob instead (Genesis 29). Jacob completed a full bridal week with Leah before his father-in-law gave him Rachel as his second wife. Leah and Rachel, like other wives in that polygamist society, had to share their husband, with a virtual tug-of-war over who got to sleep with him on a given night. It was a vicious cycle of jealousy, anger, insecurity, and sorrow.

God does not want any of us to be tormented by insecurity. We cannot control our husbands' thoughts and emotions, but here are some things we *can* do, as outlined by Army wife Sarah Ball.

1. Pray for his strength, courage, a mind grounded in God's Word, and loyalty of heart and emotions (both to God and to you).

2. Encourage and build him up with your words and actions. Let him know how much you love and respect him.

3. Be the beautiful woman he fell in love with. He loves you for your inner and outer beauty—don't let your fears and the struggles of separation distort who God made you to be.

4. Entrust him to God. Ultimately, we place our husbands' physical well-being in God's hands each time they walk out the door. Their emotional well-being (and ours!) is another thing we must place in God's hands and trust Him to guard.

"Only when I finally released my husband to God did I truly find freedom from insecurity and suspicion," says Katherine. "If we are looking for our self-worth to come from our husbands, we will constantly be disappointed, because they are humans—who are imperfect. As wives, we can't be constantly waiting and watching for them to fail. Instead, love your husband unconditionally and you will find him returning the same love—and both of you will have security and communion that you would have never imagined possible!"[2]

Ask

How can I show my husband respect today?
Where do I find my self-worth?

Pray

Lord, help me place my confidence in who I am in Christ. Show me how to love and respect my husband the way You want me to, and please guard both of our minds and hearts from lies and temptations. In Jesus' Name, Amen.

by Rebekah Benimoff

THE ROARING Lion

Cast all your anxiety on [God] because he cares for you. Be self-controlled and alert. Your enemy the devil prowls around like a roaring lion looking for someone to devour.
1 PETER 5:7–8

HOW DOES THE ENEMY devour us? Any way he can, really. I have noticed that if I am not casting all my anxiety on God, I am in danger of being devoured.

When my husband, Roger, and I attended a retreat for wounded warriors, he was overwhelmed with grief over all that soldiers and their families have suffered. As a veteran Army chaplain with PTSD himself, his own personal losses were brought to the surface along with PTSD symptoms that had been building in recent months.

The first day that Roger could not bear to get out of bed (while we were still on the retreat), I was afraid to leave him and go lead the morning share time. I was overcome with fear that he might take his life while I was gone. I was very much in danger of being devoured. I prayed, and heard the Lord say, "Trust me." I needed to take care of that commitment, and let God take care of my husband. I had to renounce that overwhelming fear and picture nailing it to the cross. Then I had to meet God at the altar with my husband—and with his very life.

Military wives, we all need to watch carefully for the enemy and recognize his tactics. Be alert for thoughts that crowd out the peace of God in your minds and heart. Cast those cares on God instead of trying to carry them yourself.

When we read on in 1 Peter 5, verses 9–10 can spur us on to resist the enemy. "Resist him, standing firm in the faith, because you know that the family of believers throughout the world is undergoing the same kind of sufferings. And the God of all grace, who called you to his eternal glory in Christ, after you have suffered a little while, will himself restore you and make you strong, firm and steadfast."

When we choose to trust God with our anxieties, He will empower us. He will not just give us strength; He will *BE* our strength as we walk the road set before us.

So let us *choose* to trust, for it must be a conscious decision. Let's choose to take the hard things to Him, as well as all the unknowns of the future. When we choose to trust Him, we are also choosing hope (Jeremiah 29:11). We are choosing to walk in His plans and purposes. And we are also choosing NOT to be devoured.

May we walk where He calls, turning our eyes away from the enemy's teeth, fixing our eyes on Jesus, and casting our cares on Him.

Ask

How does Satan try to devour me?
What is one Scripture verse I can claim next time
I notice my thoughts spiraling downward?

Pray

Lord, thank You for your promise to restore me, and to make me strong, firm, and steadfast. Help me continually cast my cares upon You and resist Satan's efforts to devour me. I know it is not in my own strength, Lord, but in Yours. In Jesus' Name, Amen.

by Claire Shackelford

ANTICIPATORY *Grief*

We demolish arguments and every pretension that sets itself up against the knowledge of God, and we take captive every thought to make it obedient to Christ.
2 CORINTHIANS 10:5

THOSE OF YOU who have been through a deployment know how it goes. You are standing in the shower at six in the morning when suddenly the thought enters your mind "What if I get the call today?" You are grocery shopping in the produce aisle when your mind flashes to funeral arrangements.

This is anticipatory grief—a grief reaction to a loss that is *anticipated but not necessarily realized*. It's a form of intense worry—worry that something *might* happen that would cause you to grieve. Anticipatory grief can be paralyzing—so how do we deal with it?

The answer is in 2 Corinthians 10:3–5: "For though we live in the world, we do not wage war as the world does. The weapons we fight with are not the weapons of the world. On the contrary, they have divine power to demolish strongholds. We demolish arguments and every pretension that sets itself up against the knowledge of God, and we take captive every thought to make it obedient to Christ."

How do we make our thoughts obedient to Christ? Paul gives us clues in Philippians 4:6–9: "Do not be anxious about anything, but in everything, by prayer and petition, with thanksgiving, present your requests to God. And the peace of God, which transcends all understanding, will guard your hearts and your minds in Christ Jesus. Finally, brothers and sisters, whatever is true, whatever is noble, whatever is right, whatever is pure, whatever is lovely, whatever is admirable—if anything is excellent or praiseworthy—think about such things. Whatever you have learned or received or heard from me, or seen in me—put it into practice. And the God of peace will be with you."

When you are tempted to indulge in worry and fear about your service member, ask yourself these questions: Is it true? Is it noble? Is it right? Is it pure? Is it lovely? Is it admirable? Is it excellent or praiseworthy?

Fill your thought life with things that pass the test. For example, along with focus on Scripture, I would also think of the day I married my husband and how much I love him. I would think of the day my children were born, my church family, and how blessed I am to be an American.

I do not want to be held captive by my own fear and thought life, but rather I want to live in that freedom and victory that belongs to a child of the living God, through the saving grace of our Lord Jesus! Through Him I am the captor—not the captive—of anticipatory grief!

Ask

How often do I indulge in anticipatory grief?
Which Scriptures or thoughts can I dwell on instead?

Pray

Lord, You know how hard it is for me not to ask the "what if" questions. Help me take those thoughts captive to You by replacing them with the truths of Your Word, and by dwelling on "what is" instead. As I cast aside my anxiety, I trust You to fill me with Your peace. In Jesus' Name, Amen.

by Sherry Lightner and Jocelyn Green

FILLING THE *Void*

Be filled with the Spirit.
EPHESIANS 5:18B

★ ★ ★

THE EMPTY CHAIR at the dinner table. The cold, unruffled side of the bed. The silence hanging heavily in the air. No doubt about it, when your husband is gone, he leaves an empty space—both in your home and in your heart. The question is, how do you fill it?

I (Sherry) have seen young ladies getting married, and days later their new husbands get deployed. Many of them long to have a family, hoping to fill the void in their hearts as they endure the loneliness of deployment. My heart aches for them. But I realize that conceiving a child does not fill the void within us. I tried it.

In the midst of my struggle to accept God's plan for me to be a military wife, I gained an insatiable desire to have a fourth child to fill the emptiness within. My husband did not share this same desire. We both believed that having children would not mend marriages—but still, my desire did not relent. I was like Paul when he said, "For what I want to do I do not do but what I hate I do" (Romans 7:15).

We did have a fourth child, and of course we both consider him a gift. But my decision to have another baby for the wrong reason caused great harm to my marriage. My husband forgave me, but having another baby did not fill the aching emptiness I felt in my early years of being a military wife. Only the Lord can truly fill that void. That is His place and purpose.

Maybe you feel an emptiness in your heart even when your husband is home. The same reason still applies: That hole in your heart is a God-shaped hole. Cindi McMenamin explains it like this:

> God knew good and well that men in and of themselves would not be able to completely fill our emotional tank. In fact, I think He was planning on it. I think by making us with needs that only He could fill, He was reserving a place in our hearts for Him alone. Perhaps He was placing in us a well so deep that only He could fill it, and that way, married or not, we would be neither content nor complete until we were in close relationship with Him.[3]

Satan would love for you to fill that well with absolutely *anything* other than God. For you, maybe it isn't a baby, but something else that seems to promise complete satisfaction. Maybe it's even "service" to God, but if you're so busy serving that you have no time for a close relationship with Jesus, it still falls short, and Satan still wins. Be filled with the Lord instead, and experience the fullness of life in Him (John 10:10).

Ask

Am I trying to fill my needs with something other than Christ?
How can I make more time to worship God
and meditate on His Word?

Pray

Lord, it's so easy for me to want to fill my emptiness with what the world says will work. Instead, make me hunger and thirst after You (Psalm 42:1) and find complete satisfaction in Your love. In Jesus' Name, Amen.

by Rebekah Benimoff

WHEN *Fear* ATTACKS

You, O Lord, keep my lamp burning; my God turns my darkness into light. With your help I can advance against a troop; with my God I can scale a wall. As for God, his way is perfect; the word of the Lord is flawless. He is a shield for all who take refuge in him. For who is God besides the Lord? And who is the Rock except our God?

PSALM 18:28–31

IN ONE AFTERNOON, two families on our block were notified that their loved ones had been killed in action. The next day, a third notification followed. Our entire neighborhood was rocked by the news, and even those who did not know the families well were dealing with the aftershocks. With so much loss, questioning was natural. There was much grief around me, and for many, fear followed fast on the heels of this news.

In the aftermath of shock and loss the enemy can creep into the natural grieving process and, if we are not aware, render us helpless. But if the Lord is our stronghold, and we are secure in Him, we can call on His protection and His strength as we wage war on fear.

God has given us weapons for spiritual warfare, and armor to guard against attacks. Second Corinthians 10:3–4 tells us that though we live in the world, we do not wage war as the world does. No, God has given us weapons that "have divine power to demolish strongholds." Verse 5 goes on to tell us that

"We demolish arguments and every pretension that sets itself up against the knowledge of God, and we take captive every thought to make it obedient to Christ."

Do not simply "deal" with fear; wage war on it, taking captive any thought that is contrary to God's purposes! The Sword of the Spirit is the Word of God (Ephesians 6), so when fears abound it is wise to open your Bible, draw your Sword, and defend your mind against the enemy's lies—and half-truths, too.

I have found that praying Scripture is a great tool; and when battling fear I am often drawn into the Psalms. One of my favorite passages is Psalm 18:28–31.

You can hold God at arm's length and blame Him for what is happening, or you can allow Him to draw near, place His arms around you, and hold you every step of the way. Sometimes we do a little of both—we only let Him come so close before drawing back because we are holding Him responsible, or feeling a lack of trust.

Whatever you are dealing with, know that God is there, wanting to carry you through. In the face of loss or struggle, it is natural to ask, "Why?," and God allows us to be honest with Him where we are. I have found that despite my questions, He wants to journey with me—if only I will allow Him to.

Ask

How do you respond to fear?
Are you moving toward God, or away?

Pray

Loving Heavenly Father, in times when I struggle to make sense out of chaos, teach me to draw into Your presence and find comfort in You. In Jesus' Name, Amen.

by Angela Caban

THE PURSUIT OF *Peace*

Do not be anxious about anything, but in everything, by prayer and petition, with thanksgiving, present your requests to God. And the peace of God, which transcends all understanding, will guard your hearts and your minds in Christ Jesus.

PHILIPPIANS 4:6–7

DURING MY HUSBAND'S first deployment, I slept an overall amount of ten hours in the first few weeks. I simply could not get over the constant anxiety that overcame my body at night knowing that I was safe, and my husband was not. Worry overwhelmed me to the point I could not shut my eyes or feel peace at night.

I found myself surfing the Internet, and watching television until all hours of the night. When I finally felt that hint of tiredness, I would lie down to close my eyes, but just an hour later the alarm would go off and there was the start of yet another day, but did my day ever end? The anxiety was never-ending, and circled its way around my day.

One definition for worry is "to torment oneself with disturbing thoughts." What an adequate description for the military wife's experience. Joyce Meyer calls it "a satanic attack on your mind," which we as Christians don't need to tolerate.[4]

Only when we open ourselves up to God completely, meditating on Him rather than on our troubles, can we find any relief. "You will keep in perfect peace those whose minds are steadfast, because they trust in you" (Isaiah 26:3). God helped me to feel peace with myself, especially at night when I needed it the most.

Jesus himself was faced with fear and anxiety, but He did not give in. In the gospel of Luke, Jesus had a reason to worry as He was being scrutinized by the crowd, the religious leaders, and the political leaders. But Jesus knew who He was—the very Son of God—and wasn't affected by the winds of public fear and discontent. When we know who we are in Christ—beloved children of God—it is easier for us to banish attacks of anxiety as well. Jesus had complete faith in the Father, and He asks us to just have faith in Him. "Do not let your hearts be troubled. Trust in God; trust also in me" (John 14:1).

God does not desire for us to be tormented by anxiety. By His strength, we can remain strong and continue to proclaim Christ's goodness and faithfulness in both our words and actions.

What am I doing to handle the feeling of anxiety?
Am I giving myself completely to the Lord?

Father, Your Word says an anxious heart weighs a person down, and this is how I feel as I carry these heavy loads that I cannot bear. Help me to calm down, and comfort me with the assurance of Your love. Help me to not be overwhelmed by these anxious thoughts. Our hearts are not supposed to be troubled; but that's our struggle. Help me to trust You and help me to understand that You are the One who makes a way when things seem impossible; nothing is too hard for You. In Jesus' Name, Amen.

by Jill Bozeman

ROLL THE STONE *Away!*

They devoted themselves to the apostles' teaching and to the fellowship, to the breaking of bread and to prayer.
ACTS 2:42

AGAIN AND AGAIN I'VE SEEN IT. A wife's husband deploys and she shuts the blinds, locks the door, and pulls the covers over her head in grief and disappointment. If she's a mother, she might even gather her children about her as a cozy comfort, keeping them from school and activities because she herself cannot bear the possibility of exposing herself to a confrontational world.

It is true that some of us may need time to process our situation before jumping right back into the daily grind. And yes, we might even need to allow ourselves to address our immediate hurt and lick our wounds. But the trouble is, without understanding, isolation is not a recovery room, but a tomb.

A tomb is not only designed to keep an individual's remains protected from the elements, but it is also designed to keep thieves and animals out. But what if a living, breathing person were inside the tomb? A person who is incapacitated and needs a medic? A tomb will keep help away too.

God has created us for fellowship. After Jesus ascended to heaven, the early church that was left here on earth didn't isolate themselves—they were devoted to the apostles' teaching and fellowship with one another (Acts 2:42). God made us to meet one another's needs, to bear one another's burdens (Galatians 6:2). To encourage one another with psalms and spiritual songs (Ephesians 5:19). But it's hard to do that shouting through the stone wall of a tomb.

As military wives, we think we must pull ourselves up by our bootstraps and carry on, with the weight of the world on our shoulders. We smile and wave and look pretty with our manicured nails and our broken hearts.

But God never intended us to walk alone. He never intended us to be in a tomb without exits! He wants to roll the stone away and send a rescue team to our aid. And guess what? If you feel like a corpse, He's equipped with resurrection power! He knows how to raise the living dead!

Have you or a friend blocked off God's emergency exits in your life? Have you shut the door to people or community involvement that could bring you out of the tomb? "Therefore confess your sins to each other and pray for each other so that you may be healed. The prayer of a righteous person is powerful and effective" (James 5:16).

Ask

How can I reach outside of my tomb to embrace the fellowship that awaits me?
Who do I know who may feel isolated right now?
What can I invite her to do with me?

Pray

Loving Father, I am hurting. I am lonely. I cannot rescue myself from this tomb of isolation in which I've been buried. I need You to roll the stone away and call me out. I ask You to send to me sisters who are filled with faith to help strengthen me for the days ahead. Please open my eyes to see the help You have set before me, and give me the strength I need to reach my hand out in friendship. In Jesus' Name, Amen.

by Rebekah Benimoff

Surrender

Unless the Lord had given me help, I would soon have dwelt in the silence of death. When I said, "My foot is slipping," your love, O Lord, supported me. When anxiety was great within me, your consolation brought joy to my soul.

PSALM 94:17–19

I WORK HARD TO BALANCE the care of two boys who have several medical issues with my part-time work for a nonprofit organization that helps veterans. But throw in holiday busyness and a husband who was gone for inpatient treatment for PTSD, and I was feeling stretched thin. I finally snapped when Tyler complained about needing to check his blood glucose, and was then flooded with guilt for losing it.

The heaviness I felt in my spirit was not just the weight of exhaustion. Part of the burden I carried was fear. With all the extra stress and activity, I was terrified I might forget something in the diabetes care and cause long-lasting damage—or worse, a life-threatening incident.

The burden seemed so unbearably heavy because I was trying to carry it on my own. But when I knelt down and surrendered each need, each fear, and each struggle in the capable hands of my heavenly Father, the weight lifted.

Military spouses carry many burdens: separations from loved ones, managing the home front while your service member is away, dealing with loneliness, and frequent times of "starting over" again. These are extra issues that can be added to the pile of the normal difficulties of life. And it is easy to buy into the lie that we have to do it all on our own. But God never intended us to.

Reread Psalm 94:17–19 above. Verse 17 refers to God intervening and rescuing the psalmist from death—and this reminds me of the spiritual death we carry within us when we choose to attempt life without Him. Remember that God is all powerful and all-knowing, and no struggle is too big—or too little—for Him. Just as parents delight in providing for their children and lifting burdens from them, our Father in heaven wants to do the same for those of us who are His precious children. "We are his people, the sheep of his pasture" (Psalm 100:3).

You do not have to walk alone! Jesus came so that we could walk in relationship with Him. We have the privilege of laying every care in His hands, and we are wise to do so, for lasting peace only follows moment-by-moment surrender.

What are you trying to carry on your own?
Is there anything in your life you think is too big
for God to handle?

Lord, I now surrender each and every burden I am trying to carry into Your capable hands. I confess that I am NOT alone! Help me to be aware of when I am excluding You from my life. Be my strength, Lord, and teach me to surrender to You every day, every hour, every moment. Thank You for Your never-ending grace and Your deep love for me. I choose to trust You with every detail of my life, and I choose to walk in Your plans and purposes for me each day. In Jesus' Name, Amen.

by Alane Pearce

OUT OF THE *Darkness*

When Jesus spoke again to the people, he said, "I am the light of the world. Whoever follows me will never walk in darkness, but will have the light of life."
JOHN 8:12

★ ★ ★

IT WAS A WEARISOME FIVE YEARS. I was grieving the loss of seven pre-born children and one who was born and died from a severe heart defect. I was confused about my faith and living—really just biding my time—in a very dark world waiting for the pain to end.[5]

Have you been in a room that is pitch black when the lights are out—like a hotel room with blackout shades? When you first turn off the lights, you can hardly see. After a while, your eyes adjust and can make out shadows and shapes so you don't feel so vulnerable.

For someone dealing with the death of a loved one, this is how life seems; we walk around in the darkness for a while, but soon our eyes adjust. Eventually we forget that there can be light. We may even find that we like the darkness and want to stay. Trouble is, if we do, we will draw farther away from the One who brings the light. This is why Jesus warns: "Are there not twelve hours of daylight? Anyone who walks by day will not stumble, for they see by this world's light. It is when a person walks by night that they stumble, for they have no light" (John 11:9–10).

It's easy to stumble in the darkness of grief; we may blame God for what happened. We might be angry. It is even possible that we will turn to ugly vices to fill the void that God alone wants to fulfill.

Even though you *feel* lost and alone when someone you love dies, God does not want you to *be* lost and alone. He sent Jesus to be the light of this world so that we don't have to stay in the darkness. God sent Jesus ". . . to shine on those living in darkness and in the shadow of death, to guide our feet into the path of peace" (Luke 1:79). Jesus said, "I have come into the world as a light, so that no one who believes in me should stay in darkness" (John 12:46).

Beloved, you honor the memory of your loved one by embracing that light. Allow Jesus to shine into your darkness. Let Him help you grieve and lead you with His comfort. Let Him guide your feet into the path of peace. Peace with your grief. Peace with your life. Peace with God. Then you will have the strength to "declare the praises of him who called you out of the darkness and into his wonderful light" (1 Peter 2:9).

Ask

Where is God shining His light into my darkness?
Am I ready to move out of the darkness and
into His wonderful light?

Pray

Father, You sent Jesus to be light. My world is very dark; help me see Your light. Comfort me. Help me heal. Shine Your light on me and guide my feet into the path of peace. Then I will declare Your praises. In Jesus' Name, Amen.

Section Five

STATIONED IN CHRIST:

Dwelling in the Lord, Near and Far

If you say, "The Lord is my refuge,"
and you make the Most High your dwelling,
no harm will overtake you,
no disaster will come near your tent.

PSALM 91:9–10

by Sarah Ball

THE *Places* WE GO

Where can I go from your Spirit? Where can I flee from your presence? If I go up to the heavens, you are there; if I make my bed in the depths, you are there. If I rise on the wings of the dawn, if I settle on the far side of the sea, even there your hand will guide me, your right hand will hold me fast.

PSALM 139:7–10

IF YOU RECEIVED ORDERS to move to my family's current duty station, the directions would sound something like this. "Drive for hours through the desert. Just before crossing the border to another country, turn right and drive twenty miles through more desert. When you see the large canyons, take a left. Continue on for five more miles of desert scenery."

If you made this drive with your children and household goods in tow, you might begin to wonder, "Where in the world has God sent us now?" Half of the women here will admit to having cried on their first drive to their new home.

Psalm 139 doesn't specifically mention my family's current duty station, but the psalmist describes the full array of places we might go. God will be with us whether we are in high places, low places, dark places, or places on the far side of the sea. In short, the military cannot send us anywhere outside of God's presence!

In my time as a military wife, God has given me His presence and guidance in many physical locations. He has also guided me through emotional places that were not of my choosing. When I found myself living in a slough of fear, His Word gave me solid stepping-stones of assurance. Deployments took me to a valley of loneliness, but His Spirit continually reminded me that He would never leave me or forsake me. At times, I climbed mountains with heavy anxieties strapped to my back, until I remembered to cast my anxieties on Him, because He cares for me.

Just as God has been present for me, He is present to guide and uphold you through any physical or emotional journey. Psalm 139 goes on to say that God created your inmost being and knit you together before you were born. God knows every tiny detail of your being. He knows your emotions, your needs, your hopes, and your hurts. He is present with you because He sees and understands.

The encouragement of Psalm 139 does not end there. The psalmist says in verse 16 that all of the days ordained for you were written in God's book before one of them came to be. How amazing and wonderful! You may not know the places in your future, but God knows every one of them. No matter how far or dark or low those places may be, God will be there, guiding and holding you fast.

Ask

Do I trust God to always be present?
Am I allowing God to guide me through emotional places of fear, loneliness, or anxiety?

Pray

Dear Lord, I am so blessed to be held and guided by Your presence. Thank You for knowing my future and promising to be with me in it. Help me to trust and follow You in each new place. In Jesus' Name, Amen.

by Rebekah Benimoff

TO BE *Rooted*

I have been with you wherever you have gone, and I have cut off all your enemies from before you . . . And I will provide a place for my people Israel and will plant them so that they can have a home of their own and no longer be disturbed.

2 SAMUEL 7:9–10A

AFTER A SUDDEN CHANGE in duty station, I was struck with a longing for God to "provide a place" for me, and to "plant" me so our family could have a home of our own and not be disturbed.

I so longed not just to possess a home, but to have what this represents. Our family had moved twelve times in thirteen years. And we had just moved again, to a small rental property that I knew would be transitional, as well. Not every move was traumatic, but the last few had been difficult to say the least. It was heart-wrenching to leave behind friends and support systems it seemed I'd only just found, to go to yet another new place and start from square one. I dreaded facing the loneliness and the heavy burden of having a family with so many special needs and no helping hands nearby to give relief, no friendships that allowed mutual ministering to each other.

I longed to be settled, to be *rooted*. To be planted by the Lord into a place—ONE place—long enough to live and grow and build relationships. As I read on in the passage, my heart was drawn to the second part of verse 11: "The Lord declares to you that the Lord himself will establish a house for you." The Lord goes on to promise David a place to live, to be secure, and to raise up children to follow Him. This is what my own heart was longing for.

Military families may not have the promise of long life in one place. Most don't, in fact! Yet we have Someone who promises to establish us—and our families—in Him, forever. As Christians, we are never really at home in this world, anyway. "But our citizenship is in heaven. And we eagerly await a Savior from there, the Lord Jesus Christ" (Philippians 3:20). The heroes of faith listed in Hebrews 11—Abel, Enoch, Noah, Abraham, Isaac, Jacob, Joseph, Moses, and many more—"admitted that they were aliens and strangers on earth" (verse 13).

We can take comfort that Jesus is preparing a place for us even now in heaven (John 14:3), but while we are here on earth, He offers us all we need, and more. God Himself will establish our home; our security can be rooted in Him, if we will submit to His planting.

Ask

In what, or whom, am I placing my security?
Am I willing to be planted, rooted in Him, regardless of where I am?

Pray

Lord, show me how to submit to Your planting, so that I may be rooted in You—to not lean on a place or a friendship for security and stability, but rather, to lean into You. In Jesus' Name, Amen.

by Jocelyn Green

TRAVELING *Light*

But store up for yourselves treasures in heaven, where moth and rust do not destroy, and where thieves do not break in and steal. For where your treasure is, there your heart will be also.
MATTHEW 6:20–21

AFTER MOVING OUR HOUSEHOLD GOODS just once from Washington, D.C., to Homer, Alaska, I balked at the idea of doing it over again in two short years. True, the moving company did the packing, but I still had to find new homes for everything at our new address. From then on, before I made a new purchase I asked myself: "Do I want this so badly I'm willing to clean it, store it, move it, and unpack it every two years?" If the answer was no, it stayed on the shelf.

Learning to travel light also has spiritual significance. When Navy wife Marshéle Carter Waddell and her family lived in Germany, they visited Israel one fall and celebrated a major Jewish holiday, the Feast of Tabernacles, in Jerusalem. This was a celebration of traveling light, indeed, commemorating the gift of the Mosaic Law and God's faithfulness to provide shelter, food, and water for the Israelites during their forty years wandering the desert.

"We spent the weeklong celebration praising Jesus Christ, the fulfillment of the Feast of Tabernacles, who 'tabernacled' or, more literally, 'pitched his tent' with us, who was the 'tent' of God's presence among us for thirty-three years, who 'passed through' on His way to the cross, and who taught us to trust God's provision as we follow Him," she writes in *Hope for the Home Front*. "All the emphasis on treks and temporary shelters underscored the truth that we, too, are just passing through this place called Earth. We, too, are destined for a Promised Land, our eternal home in heaven. We are to travel light, yoked with Christ, until we arrive safely home."[1]

When Jesus sent out His twelve disciples, He instructed them to travel light, as well (Matthew 10:9), to rely on God to provide. In Matthew 6:20–21, Jesus tells us to put our focus on things of eternal significance rather than on material things here on earth. As military families, it's easy to recognize that "traveling light" has its advantages since we move so often. But more important than the PCS-convenience, a just-passing-through mentality reminds us that our treasures should be stored in heaven to make sure our heartstrings aren't too attached to the things of this world.

Am I holding too tightly to my material possessions?
Do I travel light as I pass through various stations before reaching our eternal destination?

* The following prayer was written by Marshéle Carter Waddell especially for those currently OCONUS.

Heavenly Father, thank You for the experience of living in a country not my own. Thank You for the daily challenges, the discomforts and the discoveries an overseas billet has afforded us, all of which cause me to depend on You more completely. Thank You for the way these experiences broaden our understanding of others' perspectives, beliefs, and choices. Thank You that You cause all these things to work together for our good and that these days prepare us for more effective service in Your kingdom. In Jesus' Name, Amen.

by Jill Hart

PLACING OUR IDENTITY IN *Christ*

How great is the love the Father has lavished on us,
that we should be called children of God!
And that is what we are!
1 JOHN 3:1

I REMEMBER THE FIRST TIME I pulled up to the gate shack by myself. My husband had warned me that any trouble I got into on base would mean trouble for him, and I was terrified that I would do something without thinking. I wanted to show Allen that he could trust me and prove to him that he'd picked the right girl.

My husband worked the night-shift in those early days of our marriage, so it was after midnight when I pulled up to the gate at Offutt and went searching through my purse for my brand-spanking-new ID card. After fumbling around for a bit, I located it and gave the gate guard a nice, sincere smile. I think he thought I might be a bit loony, but he had the grace not to say so and allowed me to pass through onto the base.

As I look back at those days it strikes me that, in some ways, my identity was found in that ID card. It gave me access to get on base and allowed me privileges such as using the BX, the fitness center, and the base hospital. All that because I had one small piece of plastic declaring that I was "okay" that I was "one of the family."

How much more incredible is it that God has made a way

for us to belong to the family of God (1 John 3:1)! As much as I defined myself as a "military wife" back in those days, I even more confidently define myself as a "child of God." Because of Christ's sacrifice on the cross, my identity is found in Him. And it goes beyond that. Because of Jesus, we are not only children of God, but heirs. "Now if we are children, then we are heirs—heirs of God and co-heirs with Christ, if indeed we share in his sufferings in order that we may also share in his glory" (Romans 8:17).

So, how do we daily live as children of God? There are a few ways to keep your mind focused on the truth—that your identity rests not in what you do, or what ID badge you carry in your purse, but it's found in Christ and the sacrifice He made for your sins. We can:

1. **Know what the Bible says.** Reading from God's Word each day is a great way to learn more about our Creator and our identity as God's child.

2. **Take captive every thought.** When those negative thoughts begin popping up ("God could never love you," "You're no good") stop them in their tracks. Recite one of the verses above and remind yourself that it's what God says that matters.

Ask

Which verse can you post somewhere prominent to help remind you of WHOSE you are?
How can you make sure you are spending time in God's Word daily?

Pray

Heavenly Father, please show me who I am in You. Help me to run to You when the voices of doubt and discouragement break through. Remind me that I am a daughter of the Kings of kings. In Jesus' Name, Amen.

by April Lakata Cao

TRUSTING GOD

Trust in the Lord and do good; dwell in the land and enjoy safe pasture.
PSALM 37:3

I OFTEN COMPARE being a military family to living in the Wild West. But forget the horse-drawn wagons and rugged cowboys; being a military spouse has taught me all I need to know about navigating unchartered territories. In 2005, after suddenly receiving orders to Naples, Italy, and landing in a new country less than thirty days later, I felt like I had been dropped into the wilderness.

With a new home, no friends, and no church community for support, I had to rely on the Lord's direction. God put me in a place where I felt vulnerable and alone, yet it was my choice to either embrace our new life or spend the next two years praying the time would pass quickly. Was I going to be obedient and rely solely on Jesus or would my faith be determined by my comfort level?

Although as military families we are used to moving frequently, adapting to a completely different culture can be intimidating. When the Lord promised to deliver the Israelites to "a land flowing with milk and honey" (Exodus 3:8) they chose to be a slave to their circumstances, complaining bitterly during their forty years in the desert even as God faithfully provided for their needs. What the Israelites failed to understand is that the wilderness can be a beautiful place to surrender our insecurities. Instead of giving in to apprehension and fear that may come with living in a foreign country, we can chose to bloom where we are planted. What better time to focus on the new and (often) surprising ways God will use us in relationships and service to our new community.

God often places us in the wilderness to shake us from our complacency while drawing us into a more intimate relationship with Him. It's easy to allow our circumstances to dictate our actions but, much like the apostle Peter, we must take a chance and get out of the boat! Faith is not without risk, and we are reminded to "consider it pure joy, my brothers and sisters, whenever you face trials of many kinds, because you know that the testing of your faith produces perseverance. Let perseverance finish its work so that you may be mature and complete, not lacking anything" (James 1:2–4). Even when the landscape changes we can trust the Lord to use every moment of uncertainty to strengthen our faith and increase our footprint in the Kingdom of Heaven.

Will I trust God's purpose for me in our new home country?
Has my faith been defined by my comfort level?

Heavenly Father, thank You for this opportunity to step out of my comfort zone and rely solely on You. Although the language and landscape is new, I know that I am exactly where You want me. Bless me with friends who have a desire for You and help us to find a church family. Give me a heart filled with joy and praise for what lies ahead, using me in service to our new community. Help me to be fully rooted and established in love (Ephesians 3:17). In Jesus' Name. Amen.

by Ronda Sturgill

THE DAILY Office

Be still before the Lord and wait patiently for Him.
PSALM 37:7

PERHAPS IT'S BECAUSE I'm older or because I no longer have the same desires I once had. I have entered into a new season of life where I want to live a more simple life, focused on the presence of God.

One of the most transformational times of study I've experienced was a weekend of intensive journaling. Throughout the four-day event, much time was spent in quiet reflection, contemplative prayers, and journaling. It was here where I was introduced to The Daily Office.

The Daily Office is an ancient spiritual discipline of prayer and meditation. Daniel and David both prayed at various times during the day. The Jews in Jesus time prayed two to three times a day, and Jesus Himself prayed at certain hours of the day, setting the example for The Daily Office.

The word "office" comes from the Latin word, *opus,* or "work." In AD 525, a monk named Benedict structured various times throughout the day to be alone with God in contemplative prayer. His writing, *The Rule of St. Benedict,* is a book of prayers that has guided people in prayer for the last fifteen hundred years.

What I like most about The Daily Office is that Scripture is the basis of the prayers. Starting with a Psalm of praise followed by readings from both the Old and New Testaments, The Office ends with a time of personal prayer.

God's Word is powerful. When we pray His Word repeatedly out loud, something inside of us slowly begins to change. We start to take on a different spiritual form of quietness, trust, and loving others as Jesus did. Order and balance replaces the frenzy and fatigue of life. When we spend time alone with God in silence and solitude, we never remain the same.

Are you tired of living life in the fast lane? Our kids are enrolled in three sports simultaneously *and* taking dance lessons. With the extra duties at home while a spouse is deployed, I used to think busier was better. It made the time go by faster and didn't give me a minute to stop and think of the harsh realities of war. What I didn't know at the time was that the business of life robbed me from knowing and experiencing what is really important: time alone with God just to enjoy being in His presence.

The Daily Office has to be an intentional pursuit. Time for this needs to be made, not found. Nurturing our spiritual growth in the culture we live in today will require a thoughtful and intentional plan. It might seem overwhelming at first, but if you start out slow, at a pace you're comfortable with, God will guide you.

Ask

What about The Daily Office might be appealing to you? Where could you begin to set aside time each day to be still before God and wait patiently for Him?

Pray

Dear Lord, help me to make time to spend with You in solitude and silence, reading and meditating on Your Word. As I wait for You, make me aware of Your presence in my life and in the lives of those around me. In Jesus' Name, Amen.

by Alane Pearce

THE EXACT TIME AND *Place*

From one man he made every nation of men, that they should inhabit the whole earth; and he determined the times set for them and the exact places where they should live.
ACTS 17:26

I WAS SO EXCITED! One Friday my husband came home with orders to Denver—my favorite place in the world! However, by the following Monday, we had new orders to Washington, D.C., and I was in tears. Not because I was sad about the assignment but because I was worried about housing. We were buying our first home, and the real estate market was wild. Our realtor wouldn't even talk to us or give us listings until we arrived in town. "Houses are only on the market for hours—and they usually sell way above asking price from the bidding wars," she warned us.

In our military-induced nomadic life, it's easy to feel overwhelmed by a move. I had nightmares about not finding a home. I was frustrated that I didn't know what would happen. Then God showed me a verse I think every military spouse should know by heart: Acts 17:26. This verse brought me immediate peace.

If God knows the number of hairs on your head (which changes often), and He knows when a sparrow falls, yet considers you more important, then why shouldn't we count on Him to help us during our moves? We know that God has called our husband into service, and we know we have been called to serve with him on the home front. If God has determined all these things for our lives, he certainly has the details of a move under control.

Acts 17:27 goes on to explain that God determines our exact times and places to live because He desires for us to bring glory to His name. What better way to bring glory to His name than to move into the house in the neighborhood in the city that God has determined for you from the beginning of time, and share His love with those around you? It may not always be the housing or neighborhood you expect, but rest assured, God has a purpose for you wherever He brings you.

When you trust God for the details of your move, you'll find that your worry will fade, and you'll even have the ability to see many more ways that He comes through for you. Uncle Sam may be the initiator of your move, but God is the One who has it planned—down to the time and place that you shall live to bring glory to His Name.

Ask

How can I more fully trust God to be in control of my move?
Looking back, how can I see how God used me
in my previous locations?

Pray

Lord, Your Word assures me that You have determined the exact time and place that I should live and that You've known this from the beginning of time. Help me trust that You are in control of this move and all of the details. I will not fear nor be worried or afraid because You have told me that You have it covered. Thank You! In Jesus' Name, Amen.

by Jessica Culley

REMEMBER *Me*

I will remember the deeds of the Lord; yes, I will remember your miracles of long ago. I will meditate on all your works and consider all your mighty deeds.
PSALM 77:11–12

IT IS EASY TO APPROACH upcoming duty rotations with dread. Leaving behind friends and familiar places for strangers and the unknown can prove unsettling—just when we start to feel comfortable in one place, we're called to move on to the next. Anxiety is an unwelcome traveling companion as we contemplate the seemingly endless tasks that lie ahead. Instead of remembering what God has already done for us, we start questioning how He's going to come through in the future.

As our family navigates from one duty station to the next, I find myself trusting more and more in God's faithfulness. Each move comes with its unique set of challenges. I find great comfort, however, in knowing God has already seen me through so much. He doesn't promise an easy road but He does promise to always be with us. The furniture may arrive broken, housing may fall through, and the car may break down along the way, but God is with us every step of our journey. He is there each time we put the pieces back together and begin to build anew.

Throughout the Old Testament God implores His people to remember what He's done for them. We often read Old Testament accounts with amazement, wondering how God could save the Israelites by parting the Red Sea and later find them complaining over a lack of food. The generations of Israelites who failed to remember God's faithfulness were the ones who experienced hardships and suffering. It was the generations who remembered and honored God who received His blessing.

Even Jesus asked the disciples, when they doubted, if they had already forgotten what He had done in their midst. If the disciples, who physically walked with Jesus forgot, how much more likely are we to fail to remember what God has done for us? Our level of faith is often directly related to our ability to link God's faithfulness with our current circumstance. The next time you feel anxious or question whether God will see you through, take the time to remember what He has already done. Seek comfort and courage in knowing you are not alone. Place your trust in Him and remember He is always faithful.

Ask

Do I take time to regularly thank God for
His faithfulness in my life?
When faced with hardship, am I anxious over what lies ahead,
or do I find comfort in remembering all God has done?

Pray

God, help me remember Your faithfulness and let my lips sing Your praise. May I look with hope and anticipation toward the future as I recount Your faithfulness. Thank You, Lord, for all You are, and help me always look to You as my source of comfort and strength. In Jesus' Name, Amen.

by Leeana Tankersley

Therefore I am now going to allure her;
I will lead her into the desert and speak tenderly to her.
HOSEA 2:14

EIGHT DAYS AFTER STEVE AND I were married, we boarded a plane for the other side of the world. I left the easy breezes of San Diego and stepped out into the hair-dryer humidity of Bahrain, a pin-dot island in the Persian Gulf.

I was the young bride of a Navy SEAL, and we were a world at war. Within days of touching down in Bahrain, Steve was back to work. And the work did not end.

Transplanted 10,000 miles away from home, I had never been so alone. However, it was this very solitude that snuck up on me and surprised me with gifts I am now certain would have come to me in no other way.

In the distracted delirium of my life back in the States, I had so very little space for God. Perhaps I didn't truly believe God was available to me in ways that mattered. I let Him get lost in all the noise of a full life. I had been relying on fast-paced performance and perfectionism to bring me significance. I was tired of chasing an identity beyond my grasp, and I was tired of trying to outrun the shame that was always on my heels.

Psalm 18:19 says, "He brought me into a spacious place; He rescued me because he delighted in me." The psalmist sings of God as rescuer, the God who desperately desires to deliver us from the cages we have constructed around our lives. For some, the cage is made from bars of fear. For others, it's anger and resentment. Like me, maybe your cage is iron-clad shame that leaves you feeling as though you will never be enough, no matter how hard you try.

As the prophet Hosea writes, perhaps God is leading you into a desert time (a time of solitude and reflection) so He might speak tenderly to you and release you from your caged living. As frightening as these upheavals can be, they are often the true essence of transformation.

In the strangest possible way, Bahrain healed me. God had ushered me into the desert out of His grace and love for me. He brought me into a spacious place when I had been living such a confined life. He gave me a chance to breathe.

Sometimes the most unexpected situations can awaken a person, allowing space for what Sue Monk Kidd calls, "the deep and beautiful work of soulmaking."[2] True soulmaking typically doesn't happen in the midst of ease, equilibrium, and balance. (That's the bad news.) The good news is we can believe—despite our unbelief—there is a transcendent and transformational beauty waiting for us in the chaos of life.

Is God inviting me into a season of "soulmaking"?
Am I willing to walk into the spacious place He desires for me?

God, I want Your spacious living. Rescue me from the cages I have constructed. Give me faith to participate in Your rescue efforts. In Jesus' Name, Amen.

by Pattie Reitz

Moving... WITH CHILDREN

I have not dwelt in a house from the day I brought the Israelites up out of Egypt to this day. I have been moving from place to place with a tent as my dwelling.
2 SAMUEL 7:6

MY TWO DAUGHTERS are alike in many physical ways, yet they are very different in others. One is more reserved, the other outgoing. One guards her heart and thoughts carefully; the other wears her heart on her sleeve and chatters nonstop.

These differences extend into how each of the girls handles our family's moves. One daughter likes moving because, as she says, "I can start over in each new school." Her sister, however, feels like she leaves a large chunk of her heart behind with her close friends each time we move.

I tend to relate more with the daughter who is reluctant to move. In those sad moments when we miss our friends and the places we have left behind, we cry together, we hug each other, I listen to her heart—and we pray.

As I read my Bible, I see that my daughter and I are not alone in our dislike of moving. God called many of His people to move away from their homes, often against their wills, so that His purpose would be fulfilled—both in their lives and in the grand scheme of His plan. Abraham and Sarah. Jacob. Moses. The entire nation of Israel (and we can read in Exodus how often they complained about it!). Even Jesus Himself did not have a permanent home during His three years of public ministry.

I like the way this account reads in 1 Chronicles because it reminds me God Himself knows what it is like not having a permanent home. God is speaking to the prophet Nathan about David's desire to build Him a temple. The New Living Translation words it this way: "My home has always been a tent, moving from one place to another" (17:5). God knows what it's like to move. What a comfort to us!

We who live this military family life are in very good company, indeed. When my daughter and I feel sad about moving, we remind each other of God's great love and provision for us, and that each move brings new opportunities for new friends, new sights to see and fun things to do, new ways to minister to others —and most important of all, that we never leave God behind when we look in the rearview mirror on our way out of town. God moved from place to place to be with His people, and He makes every move with each military family who claims Him as their God, today.

Is it difficult for your children to move every few years?
How about for you?
How can we help our children focus on the good things about moving instead of dwelling on our own hurts?

Lord, I love that You know what it feels like to move around. Thank You for being with us each time we leave one place and settle in another. Help me listen to my children as they process their own feelings about moving, and help me guide them toward You. In Jesus' Name, Amen.

by Sheryl Shearer

BLOOM WHERE YOU'RE *Planted*

The righteous will flourish like a palm tree . . .
planted in the house of the Lord,
they will flourish in the courts of our God.
PSALM 92:12–13

★ ★ ★

THE MILITARY FAMILY that receives overseas orders can encounter an array of emotions ranging from exhilaration to fear. Being assigned to an overseas billet could also introduce culture shock. The four stages of culture shock are awe, rejection, isolation, and assimilation.

When we received our orders for Mannheim, Germany, I was clearly in the honeymoon stage. The discovery of new foods, customs, fashion, language, landscape, and historical sites brought a fascination and wonder.

Somewhere along the way, the differences that were once interesting became annoying. The limitations in communication were frustrating. The risqué, suggestive attire of younger people and numerous billboards showcasing nudity elicited shock and disgust. There were few Christians, a handful of English-speaking churches, and one small Christian bookstore.

I transitioned into full-fledged rejection mode, the second phase of culture shock. Comparisons and criticisms mounted. The home country became idealized, while the host country seemed inferior. During these challenging times, God wants to comfort us. Stay close to Him, "trust in him at all times . . .

pour out your hearts to him, for God is our refuge" (Psalm 62:8).

The third phase of culture shock is isolation. Many people undergo homesickness, anxiety, and anger during this stage. Some experience changes in sleep patterns, unexplained crying, compulsive behavior, excessive complaining, and irritability. In our community, one person recoiled and never left the military base. Others came close to idolizing our home country and treating local residents with animosity. God wants us to find balance, however, and to live at peace with ourselves (John 14:27) and with others (2 Corinthians 13:11).

Our goal is to reach the final stage of culture shock—adjustment, adaptation, and assimilation. Adjusting our perspective, which includes lowering our expectations, is key. Remember that this experience is God-given (Psalm 37:23). Above all, stay connected with God. Share your frustrations, fears, anger, dreams, and disappointments with the Lord. Be involved with other believers in a faith community. Use your gifts and talents for the Lord. Engage locals in the community as an ambassador for Jesus and a light to the nations (2 Corinthians 5:20). Be like the tree that "yields its fruit in season and whose leaf does not wither" (Psalm 1:3) and bloom where God has planted you!

What stage of culture shock am I in? Am I making the most of this God-given opportunity?
Am I staying connected to God and others?

Pray

Dear Lord, help me to view my circumstances from Your point of view. Help me to process my feelings honestly and appropriately. I desire to bloom vibrantly and to be Your ambassador to these people. Be glorified through my life. In Jesus' Name, Amen.

by Pamela Anderson

IN THE *Cave*

Then the righteous will gather about me
because of your goodness to me.
PSALM 142:7B

I HAVE NEVER BEEN A FAN of caves. Caves are isolated, cold, easy to get lost in, and, should you lose your light source, impenetrably dark. Personally, once I'm in a cave, I only want out. To my great surprise, living overseas felt very much like a cave.

As the newness of our OCONUS assignment wore off, I felt much more isolated from the States than I could have possibly foreseen. As I routinely received the cold shoulder from locals, I longed for all things American. I often felt lost, literally, as well as figuratively. Darkness pressed in. Welcome to the cave.

Despite feelings or circumstances I still had my ultimate light source, God's Word. In poring over its pages, I found an unlikely companion for spelunking, King David. The subheading of Psalm 142 reads regarding David: "When he was in the cave." It was easy for me to picture the Psalmist in the cave, a cloaked figure bent near a fire, stylus at the ready, as he inscribed these words: "I cry aloud to the Lord . . . before him I tell my trouble" (vv 1, 2) David's trouble was fear for his life. He was hiding from either King Saul or the king of Gath, depending on what commentator you're reading. Both men had armies and resources far outstripping his own. So David takes stock of his situation. His spirit grows faint, but God knows the way he takes. There are hidden snares, but the Lord is his refuge.

That autumn I spent a lot of time with David in the Psalm 142 cave. Each ancient phrase became my own: Verse 4, ". . . no one is concerned for me . . . no one cares for my life;" verse 6, "Listen to my cry, for I am in desperate need." But the promise at the end, "Then the righteous will gather about me because of your goodness to me," remained remote and obscure.

Then one Sunday morning after chapel I was introduced to a visiting couple who just "happened" to be from my home town. Though I had never met them, they knew and had updates from seemingly everyone from my childhood and most surprisingly, had once purchased a car from my dad!

That couple's presence on a distant continent was a warm hug from home, orchestrated by my heavenly Father out of His goodness to me. He had gathered the righteous about me. Through providential appointment I had firsthand knowledge that our Lord's care of the faint, desperate, and pursued is very personal. He is our portion. He is our refuge. He himself will come to us, especially in the cave.

Ask

Is there a circumstance that feels like a cave experience to you right now?

If you are in the midst of a cave experience, are you consistently consulting the Scriptures as your light source?

Pray

Immortal, Invisible, Light-effusing God, I rejoice that You lovingly watch over my comings and goings. If I settle on the far side of the sea, Your hand guides me, You hold me fast. I am never alone for inexplicably, yet inexorably, I am embraced by the warm fellowship of the Trinity. Enlighten my soul this day to recognize the gathering of the righteous about me. In Jesus' Name, Amen.

by Sherry Lightner

Devotions OR DEVOTION?

If your law had not been my delight, I would have perished in my affliction.
PSALM 119:92

DURING VACATION BIBLE SCHOOL, we said our good-byes. With a full summer of activities planned, I was confident I would survive this next assignment. Having read many Christian books by military wives and daily reading my Bible, I was well prepared—or so I thought.

Suddenly, my confidence was shaken as I found myself on a nine-hour road trip with my four children to attend a family funeral. I gripped the steering wheel and prayed for deliverance. Though the Lord sustained me, I was stressed and fatigued. "Surely God is my help; the Lord is the one who sustains me" (Psalm 54:4).

As we anticipate our husbands' next assignments, we can find ourselves caught up in a frenzy of emotions and activities that leave us exhausted and fatigued weeks before we say our last good-byes, even while seeking to rely on the Lord. How do we successfully handle the routines of life when we are stressed and emotionally spent?

Nancy Leigh DeMoss says,

> Some of us have had devotions, but we've not had devotion. There is a big difference. We may have gone through the motions of reading our Bibles and "saying our prayers,"

> but we have not been cultivating a love relationship with our Lover-God. We know a lot about Him, but we don't really know Him. We are active and busy in a multitude of spiritual activities, but we have lost perspective of who it is that we are serving and why.[3]

This love relationship Nancy speaks of is a gift. The psalmist knew of the benefits to this gift as he said, "If your law had not been my delight, I would have perished in my affliction" (Psalm 119:92).

While going through the motions of reading my Bible, teardrops fell on the pages of His Word. I cried out to the Lord (Jonah 2:2), once again, finding myself at the foot of the cross, remembering what Jesus had done for me (1 Corinthians 15:3b–4). In the midst of my despair and fatigue, He replaced my sorrow with His joy and gave me a fresh perspective as I was drawn into a personal intimate relationship with my Jesus.

A transformation process is birthed in the heart of every military wife who yields her life to Christ, seeking to cultivate her love relationship with Jesus. In the midst of our trials and tribulations, we delight in His Word and find deliverance.

Ask

Do I know Jesus and delight in His Word?
Am I daily cultivating a love relationship with Jesus?

Pray

Lord, I spent years trying to hide my tears, as if they were a sign of weakness. Yet my tears are what give me the ability to share my heart and enter into Your presence. Thank You, Lord, for Your gift of life through Your Son Jesus and for drawing me into a personal relationship with You. In the midst of my daily struggles, help me to take time to sit at Your feet and cultivate our love relationship. May I continue to delight in Your Word and find rest. In Jesus' Name, Amen.

by Leeana Tankersley

SAFE *House*

God makes homes for the homeless.
PSALM 68:6 THE MESSAGE

★ ★ ★

I UNDERESTIMATED THE GRIEF I would experience when I moved home from the Middle East. We received orders back to my hometown, and I naively assumed I would be able to jump back into life with relatively little transition. I was blindsided when reeling feelings of loneliness arrived.

Back home, everyone's life had changed while we were gone—including my own—and I felt like I was trying to jump into a game of double Dutch.

What really threw me was how isolated I felt. In Bahrain, I only had a few close friends, but somehow that felt like plenty. Back home, I was surrounded by hundreds of people I had practically grown up with, and yet I rarely felt known or understood.

Of course, everyone wanted to know, "How was Bahrain?" But every time I tried to put my experiences into words, I'd feel these unwelcome tears rising and I'd search for words. How could I ever express the breadth and depth of this strange place that had shaped me so significantly?

What is more painful than feeling like you don't belong? Especially when what you thought was home turns out to be the most foreign place of all?

Scripture contains countless stories of those who were

exiled, plagued with the gnawing sense of being foreign, wondering where they fit. The story of God is a story of reconciliation, belonging, and homemaking. In fact, isn't that the central narrative of Scripture: Once we were not a people, but now we are a people (1 Peter 2:10)?

If you are feeling homeless today—whether you have returned home and it no longer seems to fit you, you have left home and you are lost in a sea of strangers, or you have no idea where home is anymore—don't lose hope. God makes homes for the homeless.

Rarely does He build to our measurements, expectations, or time frames. In fact, God's shelter for us can come in all shapes and sizes.

Shortly after we returned home from Bahrain, I happened onto a group of women who took me in. We have spent the last five years listening to each other's lives, being a sacred shelter to each other. We make a point to listen instead of advise, pray instead of preach, hope instead of judge. Somewhere in the alchemy of validation and love, a sense of belonging has been forged.

Slowly, this group has become the hands and feet of God in my life, a place of belonging and comfort for me—a home.

May God be building a safe house for you, even today.

Ask

Do I have women in my life I can trust?
Am I willing to reach out to them when I need support?

Pray

God, please build me a home. May I find the enduring shelter of safe individuals around me, and may I be brave enough to live in the warmth and protection they provide. In Jesus' Name, Amen.

Section Six

IN GOD'S SERVICE:

Living for the Lord

Always give yourselves fully to the work of the Lord, because you know that your labor in the Lord is not in vain.

1 CORINTHIANS 15:58

by Bettina Dowell with Jocelyn Green

THE *Choice* WE HAVE

But if serving the Lord seems undesirable to you, then choose for yourselves this day whom you will serve, whether the gods your forefathers served beyond the River, or the gods of the Amorites, in whose land you are living. But as for me and my household, we will serve the Lord.

JOSHUA 24:15

THE SEA BAGS ARE PACKED. The plane waits on the tarmac. The day has finally come. Tomorrow night my husband will lay his head down to sleep in a desert many time zones away. I had few choices in all these decisions. Wasn't my "How about retirement?" suggestion a good idea? I realized years ago the military was not particularly interested in my opinion, but this time neither God nor my husband were either, at least not interested enough to change directions on the path where God was leading and my husband was following. So here I am, a woman out of control. Are any choices left for me?

Once again, God's Word speaks to my heart: "But if serving the Lord seems undesirable to you, then choose for yourselves this day whom you will serve, whether the gods your forefathers served beyond the river, or the gods of the Amorites, in whose land you are living. But as for me and my household, we will serve the Lord" (Joshua 24:15).

No matter what your life circumstances are right now, here's one choice we all still have: We get to choose whether serving the Lord seems desirable to us. I get to choose who I will serve during this deployment. Suddenly, I am a woman with choices. Choices I can make each day we walk this path called deployment.

Consider Ruth of the Old Testament. Widowed and childless in a country ravaged by famine, she was a woman with few choices. In Ruth chapter 1, her mother-in-law urges her to go back to her own people. Instead, Ruth refused: "'Where you go I will go, and where you stay I will stay. Your people will be my people and your God my God'" (v.16). Ruth chose to follow Naomi, but more importantly, she chose to serve God. The rest of the book shows how God replaced her grief with joy.

We, too, must choose each day to serve the Lord. It won't prevent the difficulties ahead or bring wars to an end. But oh, what freedom to be able to choose the one thing that can bring us peace, even on the hard days. Since God has allowed our struggles, He can use them—even deployment. Nothing in our lives will be wasted when we choose to place it in God's sovereign hands by serving Him.

Ask

Have I chosen to serve the Lord, no matter what? When others look at my life, do they see evidence of that decision?

Pray

Lord, it's so easy for me to despair when I feel I have no choice about the trying times in my life. Thank You for reminding me that in any situation, I can still decide to follow You. Increase my desire to be Christlike. Help me make that choice daily. In Jesus' Name, Amen.

by Catherine Fitzgerald

FINDING YOUR *Ministry*

The Son of Man did not come to be served, but to serve, and to give his life as a ransom for many.
MATTHEW 20:28

MY MINISTRY FELL INTO my lap. There I was, at our second duty station in my military life, lonely and longing for some true friendships. During my prayer time, God revealed to me that I needed to start a Bible study for military wives in my home, and so I did. It started with just eight strangers and a veggie tray, huddled on my living room floor, diving into God's Word.

Almost four years later, I am in another state, heading up a military ministry at my church. Every other week, my home becomes military wife central with two Bible studies for both the spouses and female members of our military. Through the church and the ladies in the group, we meet the practical needs of families going through deployments. Each day, my home is a place for the broken to come, sit with a cup of coffee, and share the burdens of their heart.

So often, I meet women who think that they cannot be involved in ministry because of a variety of reasons: They have young children, their husbands are deployed, they aren't skilled in certain areas, or some other excuse. But the truth in finding your ministry can best be revealed through the example set by Christ. It was His outstretched arms to those who came to

Him as He was journeying to His final destination. There was the touching of a man riddled with leprosy (Matthew 8:1–4), restoring the servant of a Roman soldier (Matthew 8:5–13), and giving truth and life to a hopeless woman at the well (John 4:7–26). You see, Jesus' ministry was not completed every Sunday during a church service; it was every day with those He came in contact with as He set out toward the goal given to Him by His Father.

God's Word tells us that He comforts us so that "we can comfort those in any trouble with the comfort we ourselves have received from God" (2 Corinthians 1:4). You have been given a unique set of experiences, trials, and circumstances that will reveal to you how and where God wants you to serve. As a military wife, you are called to serve your fellow military spouses and comfort others with the same comfort Christ has given you in your times of need. But there may be other unique areas that God is calling you to serve in. They are revealed through your passions, your gifts, and even your fears. You may be called to areas where you are afraid to serve, so that God can reveal His strength and be glorified through your weakness (2 Corinthians 12:9–10). Your ministry exists every day, with every interaction both inside and outside your sphere of influence.

Ask

How has God uniquely gifted me and how can I use it to serve others?

Who has God put in my path and how can I minister to them?

Pray

Father, reveal to me the day-to-day ministry You have for me. Make me sensitive to the needs of those around me. Show me how and where You want me to serve. In Your name, Amen.

by Jocelyn Green

Soul FOOD

The angel of the Lord came back a second time and touched him and said, "Get up and eat, for the journey is too much for you."
1 KINGS 19:7

HAVE YOU EVER TOLD a friend to take care of herself? I bet you have. But how often do you take your own advice?

In 1 Kings 19, we find Elijah alone in the desert, on the run from Queen Jezebel, who wants him dead. Years of unpopular work as God's prophet have taken their toll on him. "'I have had enough, Lord,' he said. 'Take my life'" (v. 4). He wants to be done. But an angel comes to him to tell him this isn't the end: "Get up and eat, for the journey is too much for you" (v. 7).

Do you feel like you're in a desert and you have had as much as you can possibly take? The angel's advice applies to us as well: Sometimes, the journey really is too much, and to make it through, we need to eat. We need nourishment, both physical and spiritual.

If you want to sustain your energy for your life of serving God, your family, and your country, soul food should be part of your regular diet—not reserved for when you want to die! Here are a few ingredients:

Rest: God created a day of rest not for His sake, but for ours. Our bodies and spirits need regular breaks from work. Jesus did not heal every sick person and we do not have to join every committee. Psalm 23:2–3a says: "He makes me lie down in green pastures, he leads me beside quiet waters, he restores my soul." Lying down (and sleeping!) restores the soul.

Time in God's Word and in prayer: As Jesus tells us in Matthew 4:4, God's Word nourishes us as much as bread. And, as the lamp to our feet (Psalm 119:105), shows us what to do next, one small step at a time. We are to pour out our hearts to God, for He is our refuge (Psalm 62:8).

Whatever it is that refreshes you: It could be listening to music, having coffee with a friend, getting a massage, or spending time in nature. Army veteran's wife Rebekah Benimoff says, "Sometimes I walk down the middle of the street and look up at the leafy arches that reach across the street and meet above. Seeing the trees on either side of the divide, reaching toward each other, reminds me of how the Lord reaches out to me. He too, seeks to connect. There is a peace that comes when I get out in nature and breathe deeply of the Lord's handiwork."

The next time a friend tells you to get up and eat because the journey is just too hard, take that angelic advice, and feed your soul.

Ask

How can I create more time for rest in my schedule? What one thing can I do this week that will refresh and nourish my soul?

Pray

Lord, thank You for offering me the food my soul requires for the journey. Help me to make spiritual nourishment a staple of my diet—without feeling guilty for taking care of myself. I know that if I am not well, I won't be able to serve anyone else either. In Jesus' Name, Amen.

by Sherry Lightner

AN ORDINARY MILITARY *Wife*

He lifted me out of the slimy pit, out of the mud and mire; he set my feet on a rock and gave me a firm place to stand.
PSALM 40:2

IT WAS JANUARY 2007—only days after my husband left for his Warrant Officer Basic Course, when I plummeted into a pit of despair from loneliness and isolation. The agony of this pit mirrored the emotions I felt when I realized I was separated from God, so long ago, an emptiness I thought I'd never experience again. My isolation left me vulnerable to Satan's deceptive schemes to believe no one could possibly understand what I was going through. Furthermore, my husband served in the Army National Guard, and I had no close military friends who could encourage me through the truth of God's Word.

In a puddle of tears with nowhere to go but to the feet of Jesus, I cried out His name. He lifted me out of the slimy pit, set my feet on a rock, and gave me a place to stand (Psalm 40:2). He restored me and made me strong, firm, and steadfast (1 Peter 5:10). With His mercy and overflowing compassion, He replaced my loneliness with a sweet intimate relationship with Himself. He saved me (Psalm 116:6).

Through this restoration process, the Lord began preparing my heart for ministry, as I clung to the Scriptures and read many biblically based books written by seasoned military wives. Out of my desperate need for companionship and encouragement, the Lord took my many weaknesses, and gave me a desire to reach out to others for eternal purposes.

In the book of Acts, Ananias placed his hands on Saul, as the Lord requested, so that Saul would be able to see and be filled with the Holy Spirit. After regaining his strength, Saul went on to preach in the synagogues, proving Jesus was the Christ (Acts 9:17–19). The Lord took a sinful, broken, ordinary man, filled him with His Holy Spirit, and used him for eternal purposes.

Have you ever thought God would desire to use an ordinary military wife like you to make a difference in someone's life? Struggles with loneliness, isolation, and discouragement do not disqualify us! As we yield our lives completely to the Lord, allowing Him to fill us with His Holy Spirit through His Word, God will be able to use us as He divinely planned. The Lord invites each of us to join Him where He is working.

Ask

Have you accepted the Lord's invitation to join Him in His work?
Are there some areas of your life hindering you from experiencing God's best? What are those areas?

Pray

Lord, thank You for filling the void of loneliness and meeting my greater need through Your Son, Jesus. Thank You for desiring to use me, an ordinary sinful military wife, to impact the world for Christ. I am humbled. Reveal to me any areas of my life that could be hindering me from experiencing an intimate relationship with You, Lord. May the world always see the reflection of Jesus in me, as I continue to reach out to others in the midst of my own weaknesses. In Jesus' Name, Amen.

by Jill Hart

DISCIPLINING *Others*

Then [the older women] can urge the younger women to love their husbands and children, to be self-controlled and pure, to be busy at home, to be kind, and to be subject to their husbands, so that no one will malign the word of God.
TITUS 2:4–5

WHEN I GRADUATED from college I was with an organization called Cadence International that ministers to men and women in the US military. As I trained with the Cadence missionaries (I would later meet my husband at a base Bible Study), I was astounded by how many of the female airmen are young—fresh out of high school. Many of them are scared and alone.

As military wives, all we have to do is look around us to see the many young women in need of someone to care about and mentor them.

"I'm not mentor material," I hear you saying. That's what I thought, too. But Beth Moore made a comment that stuck with me. She said that God had chosen to use her "while [she] was still sinning." It hit me when I heard that—I will be a sinner until I get to heaven. No matter how hard I try to be perfect I cannot attain it this side of heaven.

Romans 5:8 tells us that, "God demonstrates his own love for us in this: While we were still sinners, Christ died for us." He didn't die for perfect people. He didn't die for religious people. He died for sinners—you and me.

The Bible tells us that the older women should mentor younger women (Titus 2:4–5). To quote the verse, we're to "urge" them. All we need to do in order to mentor younger women is to "urge" them, which can simply mean encouraging them by sharing what God has done in our lives. We can fill them with His hope and encourage them to do "good deeds" (Hebrews 10:24). What are some practical ways to accomplish this?

1. **Build relationships.** It all begins and ends here. They must learn to trust us before we can truly speak to them about what God has done in our lives.

2. **Speak the truth in love.** We want these gals to know that we care about them and accept them. However, we must be diligent to speak God's truth into their lives. When something comes up that goes against God's Word we can simply say, "Did you know that the Bible teaches . . . " and share with them what God says on the subject.

3. **Pray.** We can share God's love best sometimes by simply praying for the young women in our lives.

Look around you today and find a young woman you can reach out to and share His love.

Ask

Who in your life can you reach out to today?
Is there a ministry at your chapel or church that would help you get involved in the lives of young women in your community?

Pray

Dear heavenly Father, Thank You for the opportunity to serve You. Please open my eyes and help me to see the lonely, broken-heartened younger women around me. Help me to set a good example and reach out to them with Your love. In Jesus' Name, Amen.

by Rebekah Benimoff

Unforgotten

God is not unjust; he will not forget your work and the love you have shown him as you have helped his people and continue to help them. We want each of you to show this same diligence to the very end, in order to make your hope sure.

HEBREWS 6:10–11

AT A RECENT BIBLE STUDY GROUP, one mom of three young children ages five and younger lamented, "I used to be such a fun person! I don't know where that happy girl is anymore."

"Hidden under the laundry and the dishes," sighed another. (Me.)

While our husbands have their missions, we wives have our own: to manage the home front. The hours are long, the work is demanding, and more often than not, there is no recognition for a job well done. Just one day of my week includes the dishes, laundry, work hours, homework battles, and doctor appointments for my two boys with medical needs.

With all the obligations that pull me in various directions all at once, I truly appreciate the perspective provided in Hebrews 6:10: "God is not unjust; he will not forget your work and the love you have shown *him* as you have helped his people and *continue* to help them" (emphasis mine).

Moms help by tying shoes, mashing peas, dispensing band aids, and wiping little bottoms. We help by showing our kids we don't have to be perfect to be loved. With or without children, we women help by managing virtually every detail of a household, by making it a true home. And, especially during deployments, we often do it all through the haze of sleep deprivation.

Paul reminds us in Colossians 3:23–24 that our every day work is for the Lord: "Whatever you do, work at it with all your heart, as working for the Lord, not for men, since you know that you will receive an inheritance from the Lord as a reward. It is the Lord Christ you are serving." While others may not notice all the work we do, God sees every task we undertake, and incredibly, He will not forget it (Hebrews 6:10)!

While I do get weary of doing the same monotonous chores over and over, I must not lose sight of *why* I am doing them. I do these tasks because I love my family and this is part of how I care for their needs. This is ministry, indeed. We women are all ministers, whether in the workplace or at home. Each of us has a special ministry in the places God has chosen to put us. What a comfort it is to know that even when we feel overwhelmed, we are never overlooked by the Lord.

Ask

How does knowing that God remembers your hard work help motivate you?

How does helping God's people show love for God?

Pray

Lord, thank You for your precious promise that You will not forget the work I do. Help me remember daily, even hourly, that what I do to serve others ultimately serves You as well. Give me joy and strength to complete the work You have for me to do where You have placed me. In Jesus' Name, Amen.

by Jocelyn Green

Scars

He said to them, "Why are you troubled, and why do doubts rise in your minds? Look at my hands and my feet. It is I myself!"
LUKE 24:38–39A

IT WAS SEPTEMBER 11, 2002, the one-year anniversary of the terrorist attacks on the World Trade Center and the Pentagon. Immanuel Bible Church in Springfield, Virginia, was packed with thousands for a special service, yet when our speaker took the stage, you could have heard a BlackBerry drop.

His dress uniform was sharp and crisp, his medals signifying years of service for our country. But it was the headband around his scarred forehead, the compression garments on his arms and hands that told the greater story. Lt. Col. Brian Birdwell was a 9-11 survivor. He should have died that day at the Pentagon. Miraculously, he lived, but 60 percent of his body had been burned, 40 percent of which was third-degree. The scars he bore—and will bear for the rest of his life—made us believe him when he spoke of the goodness of God, for he had been through the flames of hell and back again.

When Jesus appeared to His disciples after His resurrection, He showed them His feet and hands to convince them He was who He said He was (Luke 24:38–39). The scars were His proof. Without those scars, humankind would not be saved, but also, we would not have the assurance that He can relate to any degree of human suffering.

Not all scars are visible, of course. Sorrow etches deep scars on the heart, as well. Perhaps you have scars of your own, invisible yet indelible. Something has happened in your life that has marked you. Have you considered that these scars of sorrow make you able to minister to hurting people in a way that a trouble-free life would never enable you to do?

Lt. Col. Birdwell, now retired, has founded a ministry to other burn victims called Facing the Fire. His scars give him instant credibility in his ministry.

J.W. Follette wrote:

> The one who has had but little trouble in life is not a particularly helpful person. But one who has gone through a hundred and one trials, experiences, deaths, blasted hopes, shocks, and a tragedy or two has learned his lesson . . . Such a person is worthwhile. He is able to enter into the need of suffering humanity and pray it through. He can enter into perfect fellowship with a person who is in unspoken agony of spirit and pressure of trial. He is able . . . to trust God with a sublime faith for victory and power.[1]

What do your scars say about you? About God?
Who can you minister to because of your scars?

Lord, thank You for healing me, though I still have scars. Show me how to use my painful past as the key to unlock hope in someone else's life. In Jesus' Name, Amen.

by Catherine Fitzgerald

A QUIET *Place*

Find rest, O my soul, in God alone;
my hope comes from him.
He alone is my rock and my salvation;
he is my fortress, I will not be shaken.
PSALM 62:5–6

I'VE COUNTED SHEEP jumping over a fence, envisioned a stoplight changing from green to yellow to red repeatedly, and even tried to do the thing I despise most in life, math problems. All in an effort to stop the NASCAR race of thoughts swirling about in my mind so that I can get what I need most during deployments: sleep. Sleep becomes a crucial element to the success of a deployment as any military wife running on sheer fumes can attest to. Yet, so often, it is the element we are lacking the most.

Jesus understood the importance of sleep to our mortal bodies. After a whirlwind of serving the needs of so many, His disciples were exhausted and starving. Realizing this, He told them to "come with me by yourselves to a quiet place and get some rest" (Mark 6:31). And so they did as they went away together "in a boat to a solitary place" (Mark 6:32). Although their rest was brief, it prepared them for the important work that Christ had ahead of them.

The flurry that can exist in our minds: flying fears, endless to-dos, and a cyclone of cares can keep us from that quiet place of rest in Christ. It can also leave us worn out and unable to complete the work He has for us to do during our times of separation from our spouse. Usually, we are not finding rest because *we aren't seeking it*. There was a physical response the disciples had to make in order to find it and so do we. Three things were required of them:

1. Come with Jesus: An actual movement toward Christ
2. By themselves: Alone without the distractions of the world like cell phones, Facebook, or mind-numbing television
3. To a quiet place: A physical space that was stilled of the noise they had been surrounded by during their daily life

It is only after these three actions were taken that the rest Christ intended for them could be received. Usually, our sleeplessness can be the result of not taking those steps toward the refreshing of our body, soul, and mind. If you find yourself struggling with sweet slumber, look at those areas again so you can serve in a refreshed way.

Come: Am I going to Christ with my fears, to-dos, or cares, or am I trying to solve them on my own strength and my own accord when I should be sleeping?

By yourself: Do I go to bed without the distractions of the world?

To a quiet place: Do I have a physical space that is stilled and quieted so that I may rest?

Father God, help my soul to find rest in You and You alone. Let my hope and strength come from my trust in You. Keep the distractions and noise of this world at bay as I seek to sleep in peace so that I may complete the tasks You have for me this day. In Your Son's precious Name, Amen.

by Jocelyn Green

Prayer WARRIOR

Be joyful in hope, patient in affliction, faithful in prayer.
ROMANS 12:12

YELLOW RIBBONS HUG TREES on the front lawns. Bumper stickers proclaim support for the troops. Care packages bring pieces of home to foreign lands. But perhaps the most important way those on the home front can support their deployed loved ones is through the ministry of prayer.

Prayer is a way for us to touch the lives of those we cannot physically reach (2 Corinthians 9:14), but it also alleviates our own troubled spirits (Philippians 4:6). In fact, in both Romans 12:12 and 1 Thessalonians 5:16–17, we are told to be joyful and to pray continually. Our ability to be joyful greatly increases when we bring our requests to God in prayer.

The Bible tells us that the Lord's ears are attentive to the prayers of the righteous (1 Peter 3:12) and that those prayers are powerful and effective (James 5:16). So what are you praying for? Army Chaplain (Maj.) Scott Koeman[2] offers these suggestions:

- Pray that he would have the peace of Christ with him—especially if he travels outside of his Forward Operating Base.
- Pray that he will depend on the love of God to keep him from bitterness at others (who needlessly make life difficult for their subordinates, especially when they aren't the most competent leader).

• Pray for his spiritual and emotional resiliency so that regardless of what he faces, he will be able to manage the challenges.

• Pray for protection. "As the mountains surround Jerusalem, so the Lord surrounds his people both now and forevermore" (Psalm 125:2).

• Pray that he will be vigilant if he is called upon to fire on the enemy. "Praise be to the Lord my Rock, who trains my hands for war, my fingers for battle" (Psalm 144:1).

• Pray that the enemy will be turned back. "May all who seek to take my life be put to shame and confusion; may all who desire my ruin be turned back in disgrace" (Psalm 40:14).

• Pray that he will be fulfilled in his job. Without purpose, time out here is extremely long and difficult.

• Pray that he will resist lowering himself to low levels of conversations and instead seek to be an example of goodness and righteousness.

• Pray that he finds "good and solid" Christian brothers to have fellowship with.

• Pray that if he struggles or is discouraged, he will seek out his chaplain for wisdom and encouragement.

• Pray for the leadership in platoons, companies, battalions, brigades, depending on what level the soldier works. Leadership can make or break a man.

Ask

Have I been faithful to pray for my husband,
whether deployed or not?
How might consistent prayers make a difference?

Pray

Lord, give me the discipline and desire to pray faithfully for my husband. Thank You that You hear my prayers. In Jesus' Name, Amen.

by Catherine Fitzgerald

HONOR YOUR MOTHER BY *Marriage*

"Honor your father and mother"—which is the first commandment with a promise—"that it may go well with you and that you may enjoy long life on the earth."
EPHESIANS 6:2–3

★ ★ ★

I'VE BEEN IN MINISTRY for military wives long enough to have heard my share of complaints about mothers-in-law. The gamut runs from those who call or visit too much during deployments to those who call or visit too little. There are gripes and moans about in-law involvement in homecomings as well as the updates received from a husband's mother about every breaking news story that involves the part of the world he is deployed to. I've never been a mother-in-law myself, but it seems in our military communities, these dear women sometimes cannot win.

We as wives will often use the "leave and cleave" defense (Mark 10:7–9) as our rationale for our objections toward the women who gave life to our spouse, yet we will quickly forget that since we have become one flesh, our husband's mother has become our own. God's Word is clear about the way in which we are to treat our mothers by marriage: with respect and honor.

No other story illustrates this high level of respect and honor than that of Ruth and her mother-in-law, Naomi. Their bond was solidified through the tragic loss of not one, but both of Naomi's sons. While one of her daughters-in-law opted to go back to her family, Ruth responded by saying, "Where you go I will go and where you stay I will stay. Your people will be my people and your God my God. Where you die I will die and there I will be buried" (Ruth 1:16–17). What an incredible testament to the daughter-in-law/mother-in-law relationship that they must have had!

The deployment of your husband is undoubtedly a difficult time, but if you can look at it as an opportunity to minister to your mother-in-law, God can create a union between you both that cannot be broken. This is not to say that you cannot set healthy boundaries in your relationship. Asking her not to call you when she hears something on the news that is tragic about the military is a fair request. It is reasonable to discuss, *with your husband*, prior to his departure what you both would like in terms of the homecoming and have him talk with his mother about what you both agree on.

So many wives lose the opportunity to use the time their husband is gone to grow their relationship with the family that brought the love of their life into the world! Both you and your mother-in-law are dealing with a variety of fears and anxieties. Why not allow this shared challenging experience to draw you closer with her, instead of further apart?

Ask

Am I honoring my mother by marriage with respect in both words and deeds?
How can I show compassion and care in practical ways toward my mother-in-law?

Pray

Father, help me to be kind and compassionate toward the woman who gave life to my husband. Show me ways to honor her and help her through this difficult time filled with fears and uncertainties and grow our relationship. In Your name, Amen.

by Jocelyn Green

A HOSPITABLE *Home*

Share with God's people who are in need. Practice hospitality.
ROMANS 12:13

BEFORE I WAS MARRIED, I was the queen of hospitality. I hosted classic movie nights to connect other single young women in the Washington, D.C., area, cooked Thanksgiving dinner for fifteen people, and took in a recent university graduate from China to live with me for several months. The hospitality extended to my boyfriend (now husband) Rob, as well, of course. My goal was to create a sanctuary from the fast-paced, high-stress life inherent in working in the nation's capital, and for each person to feel at home and at ease.

Then I got married. When we moved to Alaska, we still invited others into our home. But when my own husband told me between two of his many trips to sea that he felt like a guest in his own home (but not at ease) I knew I needed to take a whole new view of hospitality.

There is no question that hospitality is an esteemed ministry that the Bible calls us to (Hebrews 13:2; Romans 12:13). The Greek word used in the New Testament for hospitality is *philoxenia,* which means "love of stranger." Our husbands are certainly not strangers, but it is easy to see how they could feel like guests, especially during reintegration. In our case, Rob was at sea when our household goods arrived, so I unpacked everything myself, which was understandable—but when a man doesn't know where the toilet paper, light bulbs, or batteries are in his own home, he naturally feels like a guest.

The hospitality we find in Scripture focuses on meeting the needs of others, whether that is through food, lodging, or fellowship. Most often, we put more effort into preparing meals when company comes over than we do when it's just our own family. Of course we don't need to cook to impress our husbands with four-course gourmet meals every night (and frankly, who could afford it?), but keep in mind that they are just as appreciative as any other guest of a good hot meal.

Even more importantly, I believe that sense of belonging is critical for our husbands to feel, even before we extend hospitality to others. The next time you are tempted to tell your husband he's putting something in the wrong place, or that he isn't following the standard household routine, ask yourself if it really matters. If it does, then tell him gently and with good humor, as you would with a guest who has come over for dinner. Hospitality begins in our own families.

Ask

What can I do to make sure my husband feels truly at home in our house?
What kind of a welcome do I give my husband at the end of a day, or a deployment?

Pray

Lord, please help me make our home a place of belonging and sanctuary for my husband. Especially during reintegration, give me the grace I need to fully welcome him back. In Jesus' Name, Amen.

by Sherry Lightner

MY PLAN OR *Yours*, LORD?

But Moses said to God, "Who am I that I should go to Pharaoh and bring the Israelites out of Egypt?"
EXODUS 3:11

FOLLOWING SEPTEMBER 11, 2001, my Army National Guard husband revealed his plans to reenlist and retire as a Warrant Officer. This was not what I signed up for; I was miserable. The National Guard was supposed to be safe, a mere part-time job. Supposedly, I had nothing to fear. But the sudden terrorist attacks rocked my world upside down. I wanted out! I longed for comfort—knowing my husband would be home for dinner each night—for my children to be secure.

I was caught in a spiritual battle. My husband's plan was not his own, but the Lord's. God was calling our entire family to serve Him by serving our country. I pleaded with God, "No Lord, this can't possibly be your will!" I wanted to serve God, but I struggled with the idea that He wanted to use military service to do that.

Later, I was reminded of Moses. Most of the images I have in my mind of Moses are that of a man of great faith (Hebrews 11). Yet, when God called Moses to rescue the Israelites out of Egypt, we find a very different man, a man who struggled with many insecurities.

As Moses grappled with this call God had on his life, he confronted God with a barrage of questions. "Who am I?"

(Exodus 3:10–11), "What shall I tell them?" (Exodus 3:13), then "What if they do not believe me or listen to me?" (Exodus 4:1). When Moses didn't get the response he was looking for, he changed his tactic. He confronted God with a statement. "O Lord, I have never been eloquent, neither in the past nor since you have spoken to your servant. I am slow to speech and tongue" (Exodus 4:10). In Moses' futile attempt to change God's mind he pleads with God to send someone else to do it.

I don't know about you, but in the midst of this call as a military wife, I often respond in a similar fashion. "Who am I, Lord, that you would call me to be a military wife?" "Please Lord, send someone else." Does this sound familiar?

Throughout this passage in Exodus we find God patiently reassuring Moses that He would be with Him throughout this journey. God provided everything Moses could possibly need. As a result of Moses willingness to embrace God's plan for his life, Moses was found to be faithful.

When God calls us to serve as military wives, Satan often reminds us of our own human frailty in hopes to discourage us from following God's plan. Yet as we reflect on Moses's life we can be assured that God will not only be with us, He will meet our every need.

Ask

Am I relying on my own strength and abilities or God's?
Am I living the life God planned for me?

Pray

Lord, as I draw near to You and remain in Your Word, may my confidence be found in You. Thank You, Jesus, for being patient with me and for walking beside me. May my many weaknesses be used to impact the world for Your eternal purposes. In Jesus' Name, Amen.

by Jocelyn Green

THE MINISTRY OF *Compassion*

Rejoice with those who rejoice; mourn with those who mourn.
ROMANS 12:15

★ ★ ★

"I SHOULD HAVE WORN waterproof mascara!" I thought to myself as I wiped the tears from my cheeks. I was attending the Protestant Women of the Chapel International Conference in Dallas, Texas—along with about 1,400 other military wives from around the globe. I had hoped I'd be able to offer some encouragement to these women with my words. But the more I prayed for the Holy Spirit to fill me with His comfort for them, the less I had to say, and the more compelled I felt to just listen to their stories, hug them, and cry with them.

Finally, it hit me: the Holy Spirit *had* filled me. He just wanted me to comfort with compassionate tears, not words. It touched me deeply to think that I was feeling for these women what the Holy Spirit felt for them.

Compassion is a ministry we are all called to: "Therefore, as God's chosen people, holy and dearly loved, clothe yourselves with compassion, kindness, humility, gentleness and patience" (Colossians 3:12).

Read the story of Jesus responding to Mary and Martha's grief over their brother Lazarus' death in John 11:17–44. We can learn from Jesus' compassion:

1. **Jesus went to the place of loss by invitation.** Just as Jesus had to travel a distance to meet Mary and Martha, we must be intentional in going to the raw places in others' lives as well as in our careful conversations. But we should be mindful to do so when we are invited and not force ourselves there if the person we want to comfort clearly isn't ready.

2. **Jesus listened.** And, notably, He didn't "top" their sorrow with His own. He didn't "one-up" them—downplay their pain by reminding them that He or others had experienced even greater loss, or by telling them the situation "could be worse."

3. **Jesus wept.** Even though He had the answer to their pain, Jesus did not sidestep their uncomfortable grief with assurances. By weeping, He gave them permission to grieve, too. He was not at all disappointed in their inability to keep themselves together. He did not expect them to swallow it stoically in order to appear brave.

4. **Jesus brought glory to God.** At the end of the story, Jesus raised Lazarus from the dead, bringing glory to God. Clearly, our compassion will not end with resurrecting anyone from the dead—but perhaps we can resurrect hope with the help of the Holy Spirit, reflecting God's glory that way.

Ask

Am I willing to acknowledge someone else's pain without minimizing it (Proverbs 14:10)?

Who do I know that could use the gift of compassion?

Pray

God of all comfort, fill me with Your Holy Spirit so I can show true compassion for those You have placed in my life. Clothe me with compassion, kindness, humility, gentleness, and patience (Colossians 3:12). In Jesus' Name, Amen.

by Ronda Sturgill

WORN OUT AND *Weary*

Let us hold unswervingly to the hope we profess, for he who promised is faithful. And let us consider how we may spur one another on toward love and good deeds. Let us not give up meeting together, as some are in the habit of doing, but let us encourage one another.

HEBREWS 10:23–25

★ ★ ★

HAVE YOUR CURRENT CIRCUMSTANCES left you worn out and weary? Deployments, PCSs, work, financial strains, and more have all taken their toll on military wives. In addition to these things, I've used a wheelchair for mobility for the past thirty-eight years. What I used to do with ease takes much more energy and effort, often leaving me feeling worn out and weary.

Hebrews 10:23–25 gets me back up and going again. God always uses these verses to renew my faith and refresh my determination to finish this race well. Each verse has its own special meaning that satisfies my weary soul.

Did you know the most central promise in the Bible is not "I forgive you," but rather, "I will be with you"? According to verse 23, God is faithful to His promises. When I think of this promise, I'm reminded I don't face my struggles alone, but rather, God is right there with me.

Verse 24 speaks of spurring one another on toward love and good deeds. Friends, this is not about spurring you on to *more* good deeds as we serve God, but rather being able to discern which good deeds God wants you to do. Doing a good deed just to be doing a good deed often leaves us more frazzled and fatigued. Jesus didn't heal everyone, He didn't feed everyone, nor did He meet the needs of the entire crowd. Why do we feel as though we should?

Our life *with* God is what spurs us on to good deeds *for* God. How much time do we spend alone *with* God during the day in silence and solitude, acknowledging and appreciating the presence of God in our lives through prayer and contemplative meditation? The spiritual disciplines of silence and solitude are today's least practiced spiritual disciplines. Yet it's these disciplines that bring balance and rhythm to our lives.

And lastly, verse 25 tells us not to stop meeting with one another. What is usually our first response to being weary and worn out? We stay home, isolating ourselves from the very people who can help us. No substitute will fill this need in us for human relationship, yet we seem to constantly resist it. Keep going to church. God will use these relationships to help you hang in there when you feel more like giving up.

The next time you're feeling worn out and weary, try putting these things into practice. I want to hear God tell us at the finish line, "Well done, good and faithful servant" (Matthew 25:23).

Ask

Which of these three verses is the most meaningful to you? Explain why.

How might you remember this the next time you want to cry out, "Lord, I can't do this anymore"?

Pray

Dear Lord, thank You that You are with me. Help me to refrain from taking on more than I can handle. Keep me motivated to stay connected with my friends and family during difficult times so that I can receive Your goodness and grace. In Jesus' Name, Amen.

Section Seven

HOME FRONT HOPE:

Moving Forward in God's Strength

But those who hope in the Lord
will renew their strength.
They will soar on wings like eagles;
they will run and not grow weary,
they will walk and not be faint.

Isaiah 40:31

by Rosie Williams

POSTED BY *Families*

Therefore I stationed some of the people behind the lowest points of the wall at the exposed places, posting them by families, with their swords, spears and bows. After I looked things over, I stood up and said to the nobles, the officials and the rest of the people, "Don't be afraid of them [enemies]. Remember the Lord, who is great and awesome, and fight for your brothers, your sons and daughters, your wives and your homes."

NEHEMIAH 4:13–14

MY FRIEND WAVED AT ME across the lobby. She had seen my bulletin request for office help with our military ministry. Her son was a senior, and she was facing an empty nest. Little did she know that a few months later, her son would delay college plans and join the Army. When he got orders to Iraq, this military mom learned firsthand to have "faith deployed" on the home front.

Family members often feel helpless and out of control when a husband or son deploys, but those at home have a major role to play.

The Old Testament book of Nehemiah offers some perspective for us. To begin with, when Nehemiah learns the walls and gates of Jerusalem were broken down, leaving the people defenseless against their enemies, he sat down and wept. After praying and fasting, rebuilding the walls became his vision.

Nehemiah mobilized the people to begin this formidable project with which they met much opposition. People hurled insults and questioned their ability to rebuild the wall. The people became discouraged and fearful. Verse 10 says, "the strength of the laborers is giving out, and there is so much rubble that we cannot rebuild the wall." Nehemiah, being a godly man, had a plan. "Do not be afraid of them. Remember the Lord who is great and awesome and fight for your brothers, your sons and your daughters, your wives and your homes" (verse 14). Nehemiah stationed some people behind the lowest points of the wall at exposed places posting them by families. With prayer and perseverance, the wall was completed in just fifty-two days.

Military families can learn four important lessons from this passage in Nehemiah 4.

1. Families are strong when they band together (v. 13).
2. The home front is worth fighting for (v. 14)!
3. Never give up, even when you are discouraged and fearful (v. 15).
4. Recognize God as your strength (vv. 10, 20).

Nehemiah and the people of Jerusalem put these concepts to work for them as they rebuilt a wall of protection around their city. As military wives and moms, we can build a wall of protection around our families, too, with our prayers, encouragement, and godly attitudes.

Ask

How can I encourage my soldier?
What "bricks" can I use to build a protective environment around my family?

Pray

Dear Lord, help me to trust You completely. Protect all of us with Your mighty strength and peace, and show me how I can uplift the spirits of my family members. In Jesus' Name, Amen.

by Catherine Fitzgerald

Turtle SHELLS

God sets the lonely in families . . .
PSALM 68:6

★ ★ ★

I CALL IT TURTLE SHELL SYNDROME. I meet a lonely military wife at a grocery store. Her story is the same as one I've heard before: lived here almost two years, not currently involved in a church, and virtually friendless. I get her contact information and send reminders about Bible study. Each week she doesn't show up. Instead, she sits in her lonely turtle shell, afraid to poke her head out.

I used to take it personally until a few of those turtles showed up. Each one finally breathing from underneath the heaviness of isolation she had just gone through and saying aloud, "Why didn't I come sooner?"

I had once been like them. It was our first duty station and I didn't know a soul. Military life was overwhelming. My husband's schedule bred a loneliness that I had never experienced, and yet I stayed in that cold shell, afraid to poke my head out.

I was in desperate need of friendship yet completely reluctant to do the things that would bring it about. At duty station number two, I was determined not to let my turtle past repeat itself. So I got involved in a church and started a Bible study for military wives. *I poked my head out.*

God was able to set me in a family (Psalm 68:6) and the loneliness dissipated. Fear of making ourselves vulnerable can keep us tightly clinched inside of a lonesome shell. Sometimes we can even convince ourselves that we don't even need community and that we can handle our lives without it.

But, the Bible says, "Two are better than one, because they have a good return for their labor: If either of them falls down, one can help the other up. But pity anyone who falls and has no one to help them up" (Ecclesiastes 4:9–10). We were made for community so that we would not have to shoulder our burdens alone. This is especially true for those of us who bear the load of military life!

If you find yourself without community, consider these ways to poke your head out:

1. Pray that God will give you the courage to seek out friendships and community.

2. Find a Bible-believing church family to get involved in. Then, start serving in that body. Relationships can best be formed through serving alongside others.

3. Put yourself out there. Don't wait for a potential friend to invite you to lunch or coffee; you invite her!

4. Find groups that are available on base, in your church, or in your community that focus on your interests, and if you can't find any, pray about starting one yourself!

Am I missing opportunities for community that God has put in my path because I am afraid to stick my head out of my shell? Is there someone who needs friendship I need to invite into my group?

Pray

Father, set me in a family. Show me new opportunities for me to get involved and become a part of the community You have placed me in. Give me the courage to be vulnerable enough to make the effort to find new friendships. In Jesus' Name, Amen.

by Pamela Anderson

WHAT *God* HAS PROMISED

Is anyone among you in trouble? Let them pray.
JAMES 5:13A

★ ★ ★

THE MAN WHO CAME HOME wearing my husband's uniform was not the same man I had sent off to war seven months before. This man was irritable, nervous, distant, and impervious to my pleas for communication. Eventually the medical community christened this new normal as post-traumatic stress disorder, but knowing the name of the body snatcher did not halt our downward spiral into the abyss. During those days, I had two prayers: "My God! Where are You?" and, "Please, make this go away."

As I slowly began to realize that I had not been abandoned by the God of steadfast love and kindness, my prayers changed. To my shame, my previous prayer life had possessed undertones reminiscent of Benjamin Franklin: "Lord, make me healthy, wealthy, and wise." Now I followed instead the prompting of Puritan pastor John Owen: "Pray only for what God has promised." On my face before the Lord, I searched the Scriptures for promises to pray.

Ephesians 2:4 promised me that God is rich in mercy, so I prayed earnestly with Daniel in Daniel 9:18–19, "O my God, incline your ear and hear. Open your eyes and see our desolations . . . For we do not present our pleas before you because of our righteousness, but because of your great mercy . . . O Lord, pay attention and act" (ESV).

Amidst a trial-and-error matrix of therapists, treatment modalities, and well-intended advice, I prayed on. My unremitting desire was for my life and marriage to be a planting of the Lord as Isaiah writes about in Isaiah, chapter 61. But even as ashes gave way to beauty, and oil of gladness seeped in where torrents of mourning had once raged, there were gaping holes in our planting—barrenness in the field. My husband could not remember much of the previous two years, and what he did remember was a very different version of the life I thought we had lived. And so I journeyed with God to survey the Anderson crop which was stunted by this new sorrow. Reassuringly, He spoke to me through Joel 2:25: "I will restore to you the years that the swarming locust has eaten" (ESV) clearly, another promise.

With hope in my heart I laid hold of this good word and prayed for restoration, and I still do. Restoration is an accomplished reality in my life, and yet becomes more so each day. I write these words as a trophy of God's grace, testifying that the swarming locust named PTSD has been crushed. Though I already stand as more than a conqueror, I look forward to the restoration of all things when, according to the old hymn, "The things of earth that cause the heart to tremble, remembered there will only bring a smile."

Ask

Is there any area of your life where you feel abandoned by God? What specific promises from Scripture can you pray regarding your circumstances?

Pray

Sovereign Provider of all that is needful, I come asking only for good gifts. Incline Your ear to me and hear. Grant me deep and personal knowledge of Your mercy, and restore my desolations according to the counsel of Your will. O Lord, pay attention. O Lord, please act. In Jesus' Name, Amen.

by April Lakata Cao

Infertility's SILENT SORROW

Trust in the Lord with all your heart and lean not on your own understanding; in all your ways acknowledge him, and he will make your paths straight.
PROVERBS 3:5–6

I KNOW WHAT IT'S LIKE TO SUFFER in silence. To carry around two aching, empty arms that have felt more like a burden than a natural extension of my body. I have missed a child that I had never met but longed to hold. Infertility can feel like a life sentence, a self-imposed prison of guilt and shame. As a Christian woman who recognized that my body was lovingly created by God to carry and nurture a child, and then experience the inability to do just that seemed like the greatest of betrayals. Why would God allow a loving, obedient couple to remain childless? How could desperate prayers petitioning for the blessing of a child go unheeded?

Infertility is a physical and emotional affliction, but just as He promised the apostle Paul—who asked the Lord on three occasions to remove his own ailment—God gives us the answer to why He allows the "nos" and "not right nows" in our life. He says, "My grace is sufficient for you, for my power is made perfect in weakness" (2 Corinthians 12:9a). In response, Paul submits to the will of God and answers, "I will boast all the more gladly about my weaknesses, so that Christ's power may rest on me . . . For when I am weak, then I am strong" (2 Corinthians 12:9b–10).

Submitting to the will of God is difficult and waiting on the Lord may be one of the most difficult exhortations in the Bible. In the book of Samuel, Hannah wept bitterly over her barrenness but was ultimately drawn deeper into relationship with the Lord because of her sorrow.

In her book *Lost Women of the Bible*, author Carolyn Custis James writes:

> Doubt, fear, and depression assault us all, no matter how much theology we've mastered. Hannah tells us by her life, as well as by her words, that the struggles that humble us are important regardless of the outcome. God uses the hard places of life to make us strong. By her own account, "those who stumbled are armed with strength" (1 Samuel 2:4).[1]

Even Sarah, who found favor with the Lord because of her faithfulness, waited ninety years before finally conceiving a child. God's timing did not make sense to her or Abraham, but God simply replied, "Is anything too hard for the Lord?" (Genesis 18:14). We can rest peacefully in the knowledge that God can overcome any obstacle and that with Him nothing is impossible. He is sufficient for all of our needs and His grace has no boundaries.

Ask

Will I trust in the Lord if my prayers for a child go unanswered?
How is God using me even while I wait?

Pray

Father, help me patiently wait on You in the midst of silence. Give me the strength to rely on Your perfect timing and give me a peace that transcends all understanding. Use me during this time to grow in faith and seek You in all circumstances. Lord, I trust You with my heart. In Jesus' Name, Amen.

by Rosie Williams

HIDDEN *Rainbows*

For what is our hope, our joy, or the crown in which we will glory in the presence of our Lord Jesus when he comes? Is it not you? Indeed, you are our glory and joy. . . .We sent Timothy, who is our brother and God's fellow worker in spreading the gospel of Christ, to strengthen and encourage you in your faith, so that no one would be unsettled by these trials. You know quite well that we were destined for them.

1 THESSALONIANS 2:19–20; 3:2–3

AS I POURED MY SECOND CUP of coffee, my girlfriend and I also poured out our hearts to each other. We had each been through a month of trials that felt as if they would take us down emotionally, physically, and spiritually.

My husband, a Vietnam veteran, and I had looked forward to a much needed R&R at a military ministry conference in New York. Two days before we were to leave, however, my ninety-four-year-old mom was hospitalized. Other problems and stresses began to bombard us from all sides. Instead of "Let the vacation begin!" it became "Let the trials begin!" My friend and I pondered how we as Christians should respond. How in the world do we have joy—much less *pure* joy (James 1:2) in the midst of disappointment, grief, sorrow, and trials? Here are three answers to consider:

1. Joy is something deeper than a temporary feeling of happiness. God sometimes allows trials into our lives to test us. As

we persevere through them, God is with us. He comforts, He guides, He is our Rock. He is even our hiding place. He gives us the strength needed for each new day.

2. Just as Paul had sent Timothy to strengthen and encourage the believers going through trials, He sends encouragers into our lives as well. This day, He had sent my girlfriend!

3. Joy is not something we get from outward circumstances. It was the joy "set before him" that allowed Jesus to endure the cross (Hebrews 12:2). Real joy will also be other-centered, rather than focused on self. The very people He sends us out to encourage and strengthen in the faith are the ones who will be the source of our joy when we see them in heaven someday.

As I peered back over my shoulder at the recent trials of my life, I saw something I didn't expect . . . a prayer answered here, a glimmer of hope there, a new friend, a sweet time with my mom . . . quiet moments to treasure. Sometimes it is after the storm that God reveals the rainbows of joy hidden in the trials themselves.

Ask

Where is there joy in my current situation?
Who can I encourage and strengthen today as they are going through trials?

Pray

Lord, thank You for the joy You have given me deep within my heart. Show me how to persevere through trials of this day. Help me to remember that the joy of the Lord is my strength. Speak to me personally through Your Word this day. In Jesus' Name, Amen.

by Tonya Nash

YOUR *Financial* FUTURE

In the house of the wise are stores of choice food and oil, but a foolish man devours all he has.
PROVERBS 21:20

HANDLING THE FINANCES for military families can be tricky because of frequent separations such as deployments and temporary duty. As a result, it's important that you and your husband be on one accord about the family budget.

My husband took a series of financial classes during his deployment that focused on getting out of debt, saving money, and building wealth.[2] My husband's growing interest in financial matters was surprising, because he used to view handling finances as a chore. But something about this program made the lightbulb come on for him. Before long, he started suggesting that we incorporate some of the principles he learned into our household budget. His enthusiasm was contagious. We soon came into agreement about getting our finances in order, and God began blessing our efforts in ways we could not have imagined.

God wants us to be good managers of the money he has blessed us with. The parable of the talents in Matthew 25:14–30 is a good example. Three men were given money according to their ability to handle it. Two of the men doubled the money they were given, but one of the men hid the money in the ground. The man who hid the money in the ground was strongly rebuked for not being productive with the money he was given.

The Bible includes several references about saving money and having a plan to fall back on when times get hard. Proverbs 6:6–8 talks about how ants save up food during times of abundance. Genesis 41 describes the story of how Joseph developed a plan to save a fifth of the harvest during seven years of abundance in Egypt. His plan saved Egypt, surrounding countries, and his birth family in the seven years of famine that followed.

As military families, we often see changes in pay, whether it may come from a promotion, bonus, permanent change of station, or deployment. But it's important that we manage these changes in pay and not let the changes in pay manage us. Consider using pay increases for savings, retirement plans, and other financial investments. A military career doesn't last forever and it's important to prepare financially for the future.

Proverbs 13:22 says, "A good man leaves an inheritance for his children's children, but a sinner's wealth is stored up for the righteous." Take the step today to set a legacy of financial stability for your family.

Ask

What does God think about my financial habits?
In what areas could my budget use some improvement?

Pray

Dear Lord, please help me to be conscious of the decisions I'm making with the money You have blessed me with. Lead me and guide me with every financial decision. Help me to save money and prepare for the future. In Jesus' Name, Amen.

by Jocelyn Green

SEEING IN THE *Dark*

Let him who walks in the dark, who has no light,
trust in the name of the Lord and rely on his God.
ISAIAH 50:10B

WHEN NICOLE VANDEVENTER'S Marine husband came home from Iraq in 2008, he brought the war with him. His body appeared unharmed, but traumatic brain injury, psychosis, post-traumatic stress disorder, and a blood clot in his brain had taken his mind and spirit hostage. Now battling the war within, she and her husband both felt like they were groping in the dark. Where was God?

When we experience loss of any kind, we grieve for the loss itself and out of a disappointment with God, for we know He could have prevented this pain if He had wanted to.

As alone as we may feel, we are not the first to experience what feels like a cold silence from God. In John 11, Jesus is told that His friend Lazarus was deathly ill, yet He stays right where He is for two more days. By the time Jesus arrives at Lazarus's home, Lazarus has been in the tomb for four days. How bewildering! Mary and Martha, Lazarus's sisters, could not understand why Jesus, their dear friend and the only One who could heal, deliberately stayed away!

While the sisters were in the dark, Jesus could see that this would lead to God's glory—for He would not just heal a sick man, but raise a dead man from the grave.

God always has the larger picture in view. But in the meantime, if we can learn anything of the character of God from John 11:35, we know that while you are weeping over your devastating loss, He weeps with you—even if you can't feel His presence.

Today, Nicole's husband is symptom-free of PTSD, TBI, psychosis, *and* the blood clot, working to get back into the military as a chaplain. Their marriage has come from the brink of insanity to a stronger place than ever before. She says: "Being married to someone with PTSD takes a divine amount of determination, respect, courage, memories, and humility. PTSD doesn't mean your spouse is lost forever. Please Treasure your Spouse, Darling (PTSD)! He's in there somewhere! Remember the man you love. Our futures are all in the hands of God. We make the best of what we are given, and we have to trust God to do the rest—even when we can't tell if He's with us. Great things happen for God's glory when we persevere through trials."[3]

Nicole was in the dark about her husband's future, and about her future with him. But she put her hope in the One who knows it all, who is Light Himself. If you feel like darkness has encroached around you right now, trust that God still sees. He cares. And He has a plan.

Ask

What do I feel most in the dark about right now? Do I trust God enough to let Him take care of it?

Pray

Lord, I feel completely helpless about ________. This place is so painful to be in. Please help me relinquish this area of my life to You completely. Use it for Your glory, Lord, and may I be closer to You and to my husband as a result. In Jesus' Name, Amen.

by Rachel Latham

One Day AT A TIME

I will lie down and sleep in peace, for you alone,
O Lord, make me dwell in safety.
PSALM 4:8

AS OUR FAMILY WAS REINTEGRATING from deployment number two, we started hearing the rumblings of a third deployment. I felt weary with the idea and wondered how we could set our mind to reintegrating when at the same time we were preparing for the next one. I struggled to focus on the day in front of me rather than worry about the bigger picture of tomorrow.

I confess that in my heart I was not trusting the Lord as I should. I couldn't understand why we would need to face this again. My heart was filled with worry. I didn't want to sin, but my mind was taking me down the road of discouragement very quickly. I wanted to trust, but it was difficult. I found myself asking, why? And how?

As I struggled to find answers, the Lord reminded me of the words in the book of Matthew. In chapter 6 we are told to seek heavenly treasures, to take no thought or worry for what we should eat or wear (the Lord will provide), to not worry about tomorrow, because today has enough trouble, and to seek first the kingdom of God. This short chapter contained so much that applied to this situation.

It became clear that my first obligation was to seek God

and do what is right. Next, I was to not worry about tomorrow, but simply the day I had before me. This is much easier said than done, but when I let that truth sink in and I chose to just do my best each day without looking too far ahead, things became easier.

When we worry and fret over the future, we lose the blessing that we have in the present. There is so much that we can't change as military wives, but God is more than able to work through our trials and bless us when we seek to do His will. God will give us what we need to face each day if we earnestly turn to Him for our strength. On the worst days, when I am tempted to panic over the future, I need to remind myself of His truth several times a day. I can't do it just once and have victory. It is a process of continually turning to the Lord, confessing my weakness, and trusting in His strength to see me through. It is the unknown future to me, but not to Him.

Do I spend my time worrying and fearful over the future? How can I spend more time turning to the Lord for comfort during uncertain times?

Dear Lord, thank You that Your love never changes or wavers during my times of uncertainty. You are steadfast and sure in our troubling times. Thank You, Lord, that You know my future and that You will not give me more than I can bear with the strength You provide. Help me, Lord, to turn to You as my source of strength and comfort. I pray for peace in my heart today as I learn to trust You with my everything. In Jesus' Name, Amen.

by Ronda Sturgill

CARING FOR THE *Wounded* WARRIOR

And the God of grace, who called you to his eternal glory in Christ, after you have suffered a little while, will himself restore you and make you strong, firm and steadfast.
1 PETER 5:10

THE VERY THING YOU'VE DREADED has happened: Your spouse or child has been wounded at war. You're thankful he's still alive, but your mind reels with lots of questions.

In hopes of helping you recover from your life-changing event, I'd like to briefly share at few details of mine. When I was eighteen years old I had a horseback riding accident that caused a spinal cord injury. Although I was not wounded at war like your loved one, the process of learning to live with a life-changing injury is the same for most of us.

More than anything else, I just wanted to be regarded as I was before my accident. What I desired most from my friends and family was their encouragement that my life could still be filled with meaning and purpose.

My parents were my support system, always fostering my self-confidence. Incredibly, they were able to distinguish the fine line of being helpful when I really needed their help, and doing too much for me, which would ultimately hinder my progress toward independent living. It's important that you make the same distinction.

Be hopeful. Your life has suddenly changed too. Rehabilitation and restoration of a wounded warrior is a family event. It can bring you closer together. Try to find joy in the journey as you discover the newness God has to offer. God is doing a new thing! "Now it springs up; do you not perceive it? I am making a way in the desert and streams in the wasteland" (Isaiah 43:19).

Try to keep your sense of humor. You'll be able to lighten up the seriousness of any situation. One time when I was in the hospital waiting to be taken into surgery for a pressure sore, I told the orderlies with the stretcher that my roommate was Ronda Sturgill. I laughed myself silly at her reaction when they moved the stretcher toward her bed to take her to surgery.

In the end, you'll become more aware of God's unlimited grace and strength. You'll be amazed at what God will enable you to go through, as you discover God is a God of restoration. He *will* put you and your warrior back together. He *will* restore you once again, making you strong, firm, and steadfast.

What is the greatest challenge you and your wounded warrior are currently facing?

If you put a few of these suggestions into practice, how might both of you benefit?

Pray

Dear Lord, the road to restoration looks so hard and so long. We cannot do it by ourselves. Show us Your grace, mercy, and goodness that we might grow stronger every day. In Jesus' Name, Amen.

by Tonya Nash

OVERCOMING *Labels*

"The Lord does not look at the things man looks at. Man looks at the outward appearance, but the Lord looks at the heart."
1 SAMUEL 16:7

I HAD JUST DROPPED MY SON OFF to preschool, when the principal called me into her office. She delicately asked, "Have you ever had your son tested for autism?"

Her words felt like daggers to my heart! I knew my son had a speech and language delay, but I always dismissed autism as the cause. The principal then shared why she felt he needed to be tested. I listened and thanked her for her concern.

I walked out of the building, got into my car, and sobbed. My husband was deployed and it was a battle on the home front that I felt I had to fight alone. That night as I lay in bed, I cried out to God and asked, "Why is this happening?" I felt like the dreams I had for my son were over. After I finished my lamenting, I sensed that God asked me: *Who are you going to believe? Them or Me?*

At that moment, I realized that I had an unbeatable ally in God. Regardless of what label is placed on my son, God has the final say-so about his potential.

If we're not careful, we can easily come into agreement with labels that limit our potential. The principal put my son's potential in a box, stuck a label on it, delivered it to me, and I signed the delivery confirmation. But what does God say about my son? According to Psalm 139:13–14, God knit him together in my womb, and he is fearfully and wonderfully made. Jeremiah 29:11 says that God has a plan not to harm my son, but to give hope and a future. My son's developmental delay isn't the end of the story, but the beginning.

Take Moses for example. He was reluctant to accept God's call to lead the Israelites out of Egypt because he felt that he was "slow of speech and tongue" (Exodus 4:10). God assured Moses that he would help him speak, but Moses was worried about what others would think. God finally decided to let Moses' brother Aaron speak for him. Imagine if Moses would have moved past the label he put on himself and believed in the God-given potential within him!

Maybe your struggle is with something different, such as your husband wearing a label of a current condition, or even something from childhood. Keep in mind that God's Word says, "Everything is possible for one who believes" (Mark 9:23). Be encouraged and know that you can do all things through Christ who gives you strength, which includes overcoming any label that people have placed on you or your family.

Ask

Do I believe what God's Word says over my situation? Am I allowing a label to hinder my family and me from reaching our God-given potential?

Pray

Dear Lord, help me to find strength in You when I get weak and discouraged. Your word is true and never returns void. Help me to believe in what You say and meditate on Your Word, which overrides any label placed on my family or me. In Jesus' Name, Amen.

by Patti Katter with Jocelyn Green

Waiting ON THE LORD

In the morning, O Lord, you hear my voice; in the morning I lay my requests before you and wait in expectation.
PSALM 5:3

AS THE WIFE OF A DISABLED combat veteran, I have spent countless hours sitting in waiting rooms of doctors' offices and hospitals during my husband's appointments. I never thought I would spend so much time doing nothing but waiting.

But one day I realized this time in the waiting room could turn into a time where I could read my Bible and draw closer to Jesus Christ. I began taking my Bible with me, along with a pad of paper and a pen. I would study the Word of God and write down things that I learned that day. I also began a prayer journal, in which I write down prayer requests on one side—and when the Lord answers my prayer requests, I make a check mark next to the request. It's a fun way to keep track of my prayer requests and praise reports.

Psalm 90:12 says, "Teach us to number our days aright, that we may gain a heart of wisdom." In other words, we are asking the Lord to help us make the most of our time, because we know life here on earth is short, so that we will grow in wisdom. I certainly wouldn't choose to spend so much of my life in waiting rooms during this stage of my life, but I believe that praying and spending time in God's Word while I am there is the best thing I could possibly be doing. While I wait for my earthly husband to return to me through those waiting room doors, I am also "waiting on the Lord."

To "wait" on the Lord, as it is most often used in the Bible, means to "hope, expect, look eagerly." In other words, when we are waiting on the Lord, we are not just passing time. We can wait with hope and trust that God will keep His promises and do what He says He will.

Throughout the Psalms, we are told to wait. "Wait for the Lord; be strong and take heart and wait for the Lord" (Psalm 27:14). "We wait in hope for the Lord; he is our help and our shield" (Psalm 33:20). "Be still before the Lord and wait patiently for him" (Psalm 37:7).

But in Isaiah, we get a promise: "Yet those who wait for the Lord will gain new strength; They will mount up with wings like eagles, They will run and not get tired, They will walk and not become weary" (Isaiah 40:31 NASB).

Whatever you find yourself waiting for, may you also be waiting on the Lord.

Ask

How can I find more time to pray during the day?
Which challenges do I need to be waiting on the Lord about?

Pray

Dear Lord, I dedicate more of my free time to You right now, deciding to pray continually throughout the day. I thank You for the trials in my life that have drawn me closer to You as I wait on You. In Your holy Name I pray, Amen.

by Sheryl Shearer

WHEN *Morale* IS LOW

When I am afraid, I will trust in you.
PSALM 56:3

★ ★ ★

OUR FAMILY HAD JUST ARRIVED to Kaneohe Bay, Hawaii, in 2004, and my husband was waiting to relieve the other chaplain deployed with the 1st Battalion, 3rd Marines to Iraq. He was assigned to the Regiment and tasked to care for returning casualties, conduct memorials, and counsel the wives whose husbands were involved in some of the fiercest fighting since Operation Iraqi Freedom began.

Already exhausted from the continuous news of death and mourning with the grieving, news broke that a helicopter crashed with his unit and thirty-one people died. It was the largest loss of life in a single event since the beginning of the war. Families were devastated. He counseled and consoled the young wives, some whose husbands had never held their newborn babies.

Many people were traumatized. The spirit of the community was shaken, but not broken. Life resumed, but morale was noticeably low. Wives whose husbands were still deployed battled worry and anxiety.

Low morale has become a nagging battle for spouses of the deployed, especially to combat zones.

The first positive step in combating low morale is to turn off the news! Rather than feeding our fear with negative reports, feast on God and His good news. "Cast your cares on the Lord and he will sustain you; he will never let the righteous fall" (Psalm 55:22). Fill your heart and mind with God's Word, and meditate on His everlasting promises (Philippians 4:8).

Be involved with others, especially your support group and faith community. Your family support group is walking the same road with you; they understand your burdens. In our situation, some wives met together for prayer. Others arranged to visit or host family and friends who could provide support. Be careful of unhealthy isolation; God uses others to help us (Matthew 25:31–36).

Finally, stay close to Jesus. Take care of this relationship—your most important one. Jesus said, "I am the vine; you are the branches . . . apart from Me you can do nothing" (John 15:5). Our well-being flows from our relationship with Christ. Stay connected with God, spend time together, talk, listen, thank, and worship Him. Your perspective will improve when you commune with the One who loves you unfathomably.

Ask

When I examine my thought life, do I focus more on worry and fear or faith in God and His promises?

Am I connecting with others for support and encouragement?

Pray

"And I pray that you, being rooted and established in love, may have power, together with all the saints, to grasp how wide and long and high and deep is the love of Christ, and to know this love that surpasses knowledge—that you may be filled to the measure of all the fullness of God" (Ephesians 3:17–19).

by Tonya Nash

DECLARING WAR ON *Debt*

Let no debt remain outstanding, except the continuing debt to love one another, for whoever loves others has fulfilled the law.
ROMANS 13:8

★ ★ ★

I HAD A GREAT JOB and made a good salary at our last base. The sad thing is that we spent a lot of my income on electronics, furniture, and trips. At the time, we didn't see anything wrong with it because we could afford the monthly payments. When orders came to move to a new base, we assumed I would be able to find a new job. But circumstances beyond our control prevented me from returning back to the typical nine-to-five workforce. It wasn't until my husband deployed and took financial classes, that we declared war on debt once and for all and succeeded.

It's human nature to want to enjoy the finer things in life. But doing so comes at a price. My husband and I have learned over time that things worth having are also worth saving for. Instead of creating debt, we choose to create savings for the things we desire. Proverbs 10:22 says, "the blessing of the Lord brings wealth, and he adds no trouble to it." Luke 14:28 goes further saying, "Suppose one of you wants to build a tower. Will he not first sit down and estimate the cost to see if he has enough money to complete it?"

It's easy to get in debt, but hard to get out of it. You become a slave to your debt. Proverbs 22:7 says, "The rich rule over the poor, and the borrower is servant to the lender." Psalm 37:21 says, "The wicked borrow and do not repay, but the righteous give generously."

The widow woman in 2 Kings 4:1-7 was in a serious financial bind. Her husband died, and his creditor was threatening to take her sons as payment. She went to Elisha for counsel, and he advised her to get empty jars and fill them with the oil she had in her house. She began pouring and the oil didn't stop until all the jars were filled. She reported back to Elisha, and he told her to sell the oil, pay her debts, and live off the rest. In other words, pay off your debt and live within your means.

There is a unique liberty that comes with being debt free. If you are struggling with debt, I encourage you to create a budget and stick to it. Pay off your debts, one at a time. Sow seed into good ground that will reap a harvest of blessing for you and your household. Giving and sowing seed catches God's attention. When you give, "God is able to make all grace abound to you, so that in all things at all times, having all that you need, you will abound in every good work" (2 Corinthians 9:8).

Ask

Am I spending my money in a way that honors God?
Am I creating debt or creating wealth?

Pray

Dear Lord, help me to count up the cost whenever I am making purchases. Let Your wisdom guide me so that I can freely give to Your kingdom and reap a bountiful harvest. In Jesus' Name, Amen.

by Leeana Tankersly

Unresolved

I am confined and cannot escape; my eyes are dim with grief.
PSALM 88:8–9

★ ★ ★

I WAS SITTING ON THE BEACH in Carmel, California, at a women's retreat. The speaker had dismissed us for an hour of silence and solitude, and I went out to the water to breathe.

When I returned from the hour alone with God, I circled up with a group of women whom I love and admire. We each took turns reporting on our hour. I cried when it was my turn. Tears of exhaustion. Deep, soul exhaustion. From raising my babies, tending my military marriage, investing in my vocation. I let myself come apart at the seams ever so slightly, which sometimes feels like a risk.

All of those eyes were looking at me, and I wanted so badly to let them know I knew things were going to be fine. I wanted to resolve the experience for myself and for them, for the sake of appearances and comfort. But I knew it wouldn't be true if I did. I knew I didn't feel resolved. I felt "in it." So I just allowed myself, in a moment of bravery, to remain in it.

Those girls gave me the greatest gift they could have given me. They let me stay right there in the mess. They saw me and heard me and loved me, but they didn't try to save me.

It's so tempting to advise, to solve, to manufacture closure, and therefore—without always realizing it—to minimize our own and each other's experiences. When we shovel out these sunny solutions, what we're really saying is: *I'm not comfortable with pain, and I'd feel better about the situation (and myself) if all involved could appear a little less helpless.*

One of the things I'm actually learning to appreciate more and more about God is His ability to let us be in pain, to grieve, to walk through our own valleys and dark nights and not feel the need to jump in and rescue us and shortcut our process.

Some days that feels intensely cruel, like we've been completely forgotten. But then there are other moments, truer moments, when I realize the great dignity He is giving us by allowing us the space to fully experience transformational seasons. He isn't threatened by pain. His ability to handle my wildly imperfect life is strangely comforting to me.

The Message paraphrase of Psalm 88:8 says, "I'm caught in a maze and can't find my way out." When I feel that way, I'm thankful God always allows me to just say so. And if that's the last word I ever utter on the subject—the tearful words of pain and frustration—He can handle it.

Perhaps you are singing the song of the forgotten today, feeling as though you've been left for dead with no resolution in sight. May you have the courage to admit your frustration to God, and may He give you grace though life isn't perfectly resolving.

Ask

Am I tempted to avoid pain by creating a false resolution?
Am I able to let things be a mess?

Pray

God, give me patience in the process, hope for the journey, and grace to keep believing. Show me, in some small way today, that You haven't forgotten me. In Jesus' Name, Amen.

by Pattie Reitz

BAND OF *Sisters*

Let us encourage one another—and all the more as you see the Day approaching.
HEBREWS 10:25

★ ★ ★

"I AM SO GLAD TO BE HERE!" my reserve spouse friend enthused. "It's amazing! I can't even describe it. It's like . . . "

"It's like you're with your own people," I said.

"Exactly!"

We were at the international Protestant Women of the Chapel (PWOC) conference surrounded by women from every branch of service, from military installations all around the world. Our common denominators were Jesus and the military. It was an opportunity to witness what I imagine to be a foreshadowing of heaven: women of every shade of skin color, hair color, and denomination worshiping Jesus Christ together in unity, spirit, and truth. We connected with each other in our common desire to serve Christ by serving our military husbands.

I felt encouraged as I met and hugged other military wives, cried with them, prayed with them, learned and grew with them. More than once I wished that every military wife could be there.

For those of you reading this book right now who feel lonely or isolated, I want you to imagine something with me. Picture in your mind's eye that the paperback book you hold in your hands right now is a portal to the hearts of military wives everywhere. Imagine that through this book you are connected to every woman who put pen to paper and wrote something that is now bound by glue in your hands. You are connected to every woman who purchased this book for herself, or to give to a friend. You are connecting, at this very moment, with every other woman holding this same paperback book in her hands. With this picture in your mind, now imagine the sheer number of women that is! We are a multitude, a band of sisters united in our shared faith in Jesus.

You are not alone. There are other women around you on base or on post, and I pray that you will somehow find a way to connect with another military wife nearby. But if geography prohibits this, you can also connect with other military wives online, through one of several groups of women who gather on message boards or in Facebook groups in support of each other. Find an up-to-date list of groups at faithdeployed.com/resources.

We are called to community. Do not feel like you have to do this alone. Find some of "your people." Because we're here, and we need each other so much. "So in Christ we who are many form one body, and each member belongs to all the others" (Romans 12:5).

Ask

Do you have another military wife sister nearby?
If so, call her and plan a coffee date or a play date this week.
How can you reach out to support another military wife today, either in person, online, or on the phone?

Pray

Oh Lord, thank You that I am one of "Your people"—You have made me Your daughter. Thank You for each one of my sisters reading this book today. I pray that no military wife would ever feel like she is alone. In Jesus' Name, Amen.

Section Eight

FOR BLUE STAR MOMS:

Trusting God with Your Service Member

---

*May the God of hope fill you with all joy
and peace as you trust in him,*

*so that you may overflow with hope
by the power of the Holy Spirit.*

ROMANS 15:13

by Donna Mull

LETTING GO

Now I know that you fear God, because you have not withheld from me your son, your only son.
GENESIS 22:12B

IT IS AN ANCIENT AND FAMILIAR THEME . . . *letting go* of your child for a higher purpose. With great wrestling I would learn the incredible power of a simple pronoun—*my*. I have always felt deep compassion and great appreciation for those who have sacrificed to secure the freedoms I enjoy every day. But when it was MY son going into harm's way, MY daughter-in-law and grandchildren giving up so much, everything changed! I could think of so many reasonable objections to this plan. What if it didn't end well?

In 1 Samuel 1:27–28, we hear the words of Hannah: "I prayed for this child, and the Lord has granted me what I asked of him. So now I give him to the Lord. For his whole life he will be given over to the Lord."

Was it any easier for Hannah to give up the son she so desperately desired for such a long time so that he might live apart from her and serve the Lord? Was it any easier for Abraham to lay his son of promise on an altar in obedient sacrifice (Genesis 22:12b)? What was in the heart of Moses' mother as she put her infant son in a basket and set it adrift in the Nile? "But when she could hide him no longer, she got a papyrus basket for him and coated it with tar and pitch. Then she placed the child in it and put it among the reeds along the bank of the Nile" (Exodus 2:3).

We are so deeply attached to our children that it is easy to forget they do not belong to us. We are entrusted with the task of loving them, caring for their needs, and raising them to send them off into the unique destiny God has for them.

Neither Hannah, Abraham, nor Moses's mother, Jochebed, had any assurance of the outcome of letting go and yet they obediently did so. I believe that is because their hope was not in the outcome but in the God they trusted. Did their hearts hurt? Immeasurably! Did everything in them resist and question? Undoubtedly! We have the benefit of hindsight in seeing how profoundly God used each of these sons to fulfill His eternal plan. We may not always get to see in our lifetime what God will accomplish through our *letting go*, but we can decide to place our hope in God's ultimate outcome.

Will God, who is the same yesterday, today, and forever, honor the obedient surrender of my child to His purposes any less than He did those saints of old who were flesh and blood just like me?
More importantly, will the Father who gave His only Son to die for me not understand what I am feeling?

Father, I give You what is Yours already—the child You gave me the privilege of raising to step into the unique destiny You have for him. I choose to trust You with the outcome even when I may not understand it. In Jesus' Name, Amen.

by Gloria D. Kroeze

WARRIOR *Angels*

Suddenly a great company of the heavenly host
appeared with the angel,
praising God and saying,
"Glory to God in the highest,
and on earth peace to those on whom his favor rests."
LUKE 2:13–14

★ ★ ★

I WAS PREPARING TO LEAVE THE STORE when I saw it. It was a very small nativity, with Joseph and Mary lying on either side of baby Jesus (a rather realistic depiction for a woman who just had a baby!), the tiny baby in a manger, a couple of cattle, and an angel at attention over the manger.

That lone angel was a reminder to me that God's angels were watching over that precious babe born in Bethlehem. The verses from Luke that describe that awesome night of Jesus' birth tell us that there was "a great company of heavenly host" that appeared to the shepherds. As I imagine this scene, I think of a large group of angels dressed in choir robes, singing their praise-filled proclamation of Jesus' birth. The songs that we sing at Christmas reinforce this image: "Angels we have heard on high sweetly singing o'er the plains."

But I had several surprises as I studied this passage. My first realization was that "a great company of heavenly host" is way beyond a large group of angels. A "host" is huge, likely thousands of angels! I also realized that in the original Greek the terminology is from the military. This "heavenly host" is not a choir of angels. It is an army of angels. Their attire is not choir robes but full battle array. The words that they sing are not sweet songs, but a heavenly version of "Hail to the Chief."

The reason why this babe in Bethlehem was born "was to destroy the devil's work" (1 John 3:8b). Satan was equally intent on destroying Jesus and preventing Him from accomplishing His life's work. Satan wanted to stop Jesus from going to the cross. The story of Jesus' birth reminds us that even as a babe born into this world, the formation for a spiritual battle was in place. The angels both proclaimed his birth and were poised and ready to protect the Son of God.

God's warrior angels are still at work today. What a comfort to know that we can claim the words of Psalm 91:11: "For he will command his angels concerning you to guard you in all your ways." Nothing will be able to hinder God's purposes for your warrior's life or separate your loved one from God's love. What a comfort to think of warrior angels watching over our warriors just as those angels watched over Jesus when He was born in Bethlehem!

Ask

How do you view angels and their role in our lives? What does it mean to you that warrior angels watch over your warrior?

Pray

Thank You, Lord God, for Your angels. I ask that Your angels watch over my life, my walk, and my way, and that they also watch over the footsteps of those I love. In Jesus' Name, Amen.

by Kathy Guzzo

Solitude

Come near to God and he will come near to you.
JAMES 4:8

FOR MANY, SOLITUDE MEANS a time of loneliness, seclusion, or even isolation, but I believe experiencing solitude is an opportunity for complete satisfaction by basking in peace, oneness, and tranquility with the Lord.

As military moms we've all felt the emptiness and longing that's a direct result of having a child out of arm's reach and possibly in harm's way. From the first good-bye, when they leave for boot camp, to yearlong deployments, the desire to see them, to give them a hug, or visit with them, can consume us enough to affect our daily lives. That loneliness can become depression, which results in distancing ourselves from God as well as from others who care about us.

In contrast, true solace with God is fulfilling. Solitude is being alone with our thoughts and focusing on who God is regardless of where we are or what's happening in our lives. Times of solitude can be a time we've set apart to silently listen, observe, and appreciate creation while letting God fill our entire being. Or, possibly, a time when life's crazy, yet for just a minute we take a deep breath and choose to acknowledge God's presence—the presence that is powerful enough to overcome the longing and sense of loneliness in our hearts. Joan Arnold says it clearly: "God is always present in the temple of your heart . . . His home. And when you come in to meet Him there, you find that it is the one place of deep satisfaction where every longing is met."[1]

Jesus was our example for this. Even when in the midst of ministering to crowds of people, He set time aside to be alone with the Father (Matthew 14:23; Luke 5:16).

I encourage you to grab a moment whenever you can, or better yet, plan a specific time to be alone with Him. Allow Him to be your constant companion, filling the loneliness with hope, peace, and the knowledge that with Him you'll never be lonely. In solitude, we feel God's . . .

Sovereignty
Outpouring
Love
Inspiration
Tenderness
Understanding
Desires
Encouragement

Ask

When was the last time you took a moment or a block of time to focus on God, allowing Him to replace your loneliness with His presence?
If you've never consciously done this, are you willing to find the solace that Jesus knew was vital to everyday life?

Pray

Heavenly Father, when the loneliness for my child is overwhelming I pray that You would help me find solace in You. My desire is for You to fill the emptiness with Your presence, hope, and peace. Thank You that as I spend time with You, You will draw near to me. In Jesus' Name, Amen.

by Kathleen Edick

SECRET *Fears*

O Lord, You have searched me and You know me.
You know when I sit and when I rise.
You perceive my thoughts from afar.
You discern my going out and my lying down.
You are familiar with all my ways.
PSALM 139:1–3

★ ★ ★

I RECALL LEANING AGAINST OUR SON'S solid frame, sipping coffee and watching the people go by in the airport. I was standing so close because I knew that for at least a year he was going to be far from home. Interrupting my thoughts, he looked down at me and said, "Mom, it is hard to send your son to war?"

It was as if he had seen the very thoughts I had tried so hard to cover up. You know the thoughts I mean, the ones we try and push aside . . . the ones we pretend not to entertain?

So, let's just get these thoughts out in the open; perhaps you have entertained these as well. You stand in the biting wind as you are being handed a folded flag. You envision yourself as the mother in *Saving Private Ryan*, as she crumples in grief onto her porch as a car slowly approaches, bringing news she already knows. You imagine watching the evening news as they report on the loss of your child.

We try to push those thoughts away and berate ourselves for such negative thinking, and secretly fear that even the act of thinking them may cause them to come true. At times our faith fails, and we fear God will not grant us our desire for safety and happy endings as we define them.

Yet, even these thoughts God knows. He knows how vulnerable we are to manipulations of the enemy when these thoughts consume us. Therefore He asks us to heed His Word and to take every thought captive to Christ (2 Corinthians 10:5).

Psalm 139:16 comforted me in the deepest recess of that fear: "All the days ordained for me were written in your book, before one of them came to be." There is incredible freedom in that. It does not matter if we are in combat or in our bed at home, our day has been ordained. No matter what the circumstances may be, we will survive until our day.

So, we can relinquish these secret fears and rest. We have nothing to do with the days set for us—they are set before we came to be. You can walk right through the center of the fear of loss by taking those thoughts, being honest with them, and bringing them to God, who perceives our thoughts from afar.

What thoughts keep you in bondage? Choose one of the following ways of taking those thoughts captive to Christ and explain how you can use it: journaling, drawing, praying. How does the knowledge that your days have been ordained free you from worry?

Lord, thank You that You know us, and You love us. You have already numbered all our days. Help us give to You, O Christ, our vain imaginings, so we may receive in their place Your peace. In Jesus' Name, Amen.

by Kathy Guzzo

Wait TRAINING

Wait for the Lord; be strong and let your heart take courage; wait for the Lord.
PSALM 27:14 ESV

★ ★ ★

YES. NO. WAIT.

These are the answers God has for us. "Wait" is usually the toughest. When situations occur in my life that I want resolved immediately, I'm reminded of my dislike for waiting. Without immediate answers I feel frustrated and start doubting as to whether God is listening, which leads me to attempt to do things my way in my timetable.

One instance I had to wait for an extended amount of time was during our son's deployments. Having basic communication with him didn't seem like too much to ask. However, because of his unit's mission, we usually didn't hear from him for several weeks. As a mom, that waiting was torturous.

What God showed me then is that instead of not liking it when His answer is "wait," I need to see it as a time of training myself not to act. To stand still and watch Him work. If I don't, my negative response allows Satan to create worry and doubt. By not hearing from Brian regularly, my faith actually grew because when we did have contact, I invariably saw how God had been working all along.

Sarah longed for a promised child, Joseph spent years in prison, and Mary and Martha prayed for Jesus to heal Lazarus.

Each waited and saw God's answer at the perfect time to fulfill His plan, and to glorify the Father. And just as you may be waiting right now to see your military child again, Christians wait to be united with Jesus face-to-face, as He has gone to heaven ahead of us to prepare a place for us (John 14:3). Waiting for God's timing allows His perfect plan to fully develop and not be short-circuited by impatience.

Maybe you're like me and have waited for a long time for an answer to a specific prayer; I encourage you not to grow weary. God is listening, He has a plan for us, and His timing is perfect. In *Lost Women of the Bible* Carolyn Curtis James states, "God's silence is not an accurate way to measure what he is doing. It's easy to forget he often does his best work when, so far as we can tell, he doesn't seem to be doing anything at all."[2]

The times I did speak with our son during his deployments and learned of his platoon's experiences, I realized God was answering my prayers, but chose to teach me "wait training," giving me the opportunity to glorify Him when I saw the answers. Praise God that He loves us enough to say, "*Wait, my child.*"

When God answers a prayer by saying "wait," what are ways that you can use that time to train yourself to accept His perfect will?

What are ways to give God glory when we do see prayer answered?

Heavenly Father, I know there are times when I ask You for things that the best answer You can give me is to wait, and however hard it may be for me, help me trust You. I pray that when I do see the results of my waiting I would willingly give You the glory. In Your precious Name, I pray. In Jesus' Name, Amen.

by Donna Mull

THE *Formula*

"This, then, is how you should pray: 'Our Father in heaven, hallowed be your name, your kingdom come, your will be done . . .'"
MATTHEW 6:9–10

REFLECTING BACK OVER LIFE I have given some thought to losses. Sometimes they have come suddenly and unexpectedly. Other times I could see their potential approach, and I am struck by how just the threat of loss impacts my behavior.

At the first word of my son's deployment, I instinctively sprang into action. I bought little teddy bears dressed in fatigues that sang "Proud To Be An American" with little voice recorders attached so that my grandchildren could hear Daddy's voice at bedtime. Each bear had special laminated pictures of Dad and child together hanging from dog tags around the bear's neck. I also spent hours creating a "scrapbook" with messages to help their child minds deal with this difficult absence.

I searched for a prayer support group of other deployed soldier's families but couldn't make it materialize. PLAN B: I wrote and e-mailed weekly prayer devotionals to friends and family for a whole year to try to garner prayer support for my son and his family. It was a commitment that nearly "deep-sixed" me along with my full-time job, and home and church responsibilities. As often as I could gather the strength, I would leave work Friday afternoon, drive the four hours to my daughter-in-law's home to encourage and support her and my grandkids. Then I would make the four-hour trip back on Sunday and start the next work week over again. Ultimately, fatigue and depression weighed me down.

These were all *good* things. However, as I distance myself a little bit from that year, I see something I would never have been able or willing to see at the time. Even the slightest threat of losing my son and living with the compounded grief of my own loss as well as his wife's and children's grief led me to invest myself in ways that perhaps might move the hand of God—to find the right formula to secure the outcome I desperately desired. It tells me something about my level of trust in God.

Indeed we should pray, encourage, and support. The Bible assures that the prayers of a righteous person accomplishes much (James 5:16).

We also know there is power when people pray together (Matthew 18:20). But what is the magic number of prayers that will move the hand of God? God is Sovereign and He will do what He will do . . . and in the end we will know He is right. God blesses because it is His nature and desire to bless. He is a benevolent God. He blesses because He is faithful to His promises. He has proven over and over again that He is Lord of the harvest—no season is unproductive in His hands, even seasons of greatest trial.

Ask

Am I weighing myself down trying to find the right formula for the blessing I desperately desire? Can I trust Him?

Pray

Father, You alone are God. Have Your way in my life. I would never choose the costly things that might yield the highest blessing. Examine my heart so that every action will spring from a pure motive. In Jesus' Name, Amen.

by Sharon Carrns

GOD, MY SOLDIER'S *Parent*

Do not be anxious about anything, but in everything, by prayer and petition, with thanksgiving, present your requests to God. And the peace of God, which transcends all understanding, will guard your hearts and your minds in Christ Jesus.

PHILIPPIANS 4:6–7

I HAVE BEEN GRIPPED BY FEAR. My daughter is fighting in a war. My son-in-law has already been wounded in a roadside bomb and spent a year in Walter Reed Army Medical Center. None of the men who were with him survived. The scars on his face and body are always there to remind me that my kids are in a very real war.

I pace. I eat. I shop. I start cleaning like a crazy woman. At night I lie awake, tossing, turning, and imagining what is happening in Iraq.

The cycle continues, while all the while inside I know the truth. There is nothing to do and nowhere to go but to God. Finally, my heart breaks open and the tears flow like a bursting dam. "Father! Help me! I am afraid. This child I protected for so many years is far from me. I can't see her. I can't go to her. I can't stop the evil that is all around her. But You can. Please protect both of us. For evil is all around me as surely as it is around her. You have said in Your Word that You have not given us a spirit of fear, but of power, and of love, and of a sound mind (2 Timothy 1:7).

Before you were your child's parent, God was his or her parent. He has known the path this child will walk all along, just as He has known your path. No amount of fear is going to change that path. But fear will surely rob you of life and peace along the way. And if your child is aware of those fears it will be an added burden to carry when prayers and encouragement are what are needed most.

When you struggle, go to God and be honest with Him. Pour out all of what you worry and imagine, and ask His help. Then trust that the outcome is in His hands. Take comfort in His words in Isaiah 41:12b–13 when He says, "Those who wage war against you will be as nothing at all. For I am the Lord, your God, who takes hold of your right hand and says to you, Do not fear; I will help you." Then send that same verse to your child, remembering that God is the proud parent of this soldier. He or she is in good hands.

Ask

Is fear for my child controlling my thoughts
and affecting my life? How?
Am I really honest with God about those feelings,
believing He cares and can help?

Pray

Father, You know how much my child means to me. But it is not in my hands. No amount of fear or obsessing is going to change that. My child is in Your hands. Please bring that truth to my mind every time I start to let fear take over. Take care of my child, Lord, for all of our lives are in Your hands. In Jesus' Name, Amen.

by Kathy Guzzo

A NEW *Normal*

Accept one another, then, just as Christ accepted you, in order to bring praise to God.
ROMANS 15:7

THE ANTICIPATION OF OUR SON'S ARRIVAL home after his first deployment brought with it conflicting emotions and questions. The thought of seeing him, hugging him, talking with him, and just being near him brought overwhelming joy. Yet, when it came to really relating to him, I wasn't sure if he'd welcome a hug or really want to talk with me. I had known and understood the young man who left, but would I recognize who he was when he returned?

In 2004, there weren't many resources available regarding what to expect after a deployment. However, one quote I did find helpful in focusing my thinking was from *When Duty Calls*, by Carol Vandesteeg. Discussing the reunion, she states, "Expect change and be ready to do things differently rather than resisting changes that will occur."[3] So that's what I started to do. I told myself repeatedly that change in Brian was inevitable and that was okay. The change wouldn't necessarily be bad, it would just be different. All of us had changed in the months he was away. Change was part of life.

I'd heard others say to be patient until they get back to normal. But what was normal? And, what right did I have to expect him to be who he was before he left? If he was different because of his experience, it wasn't going to alter my love for him.

I thought of the many people in the Bible Jesus met right where they were. The woman at the well, the lepers, Zacchaeus, the demon-filled man, Saul (Paul), even Thomas when he doubted. Jesus spent time with each of them; showing His unconditional love. It was obvious to each of them that He wasn't judging them but offering the acceptance and love they each needed.

Therefore, I decided that I would meet our son wherever his new normal was. I wasn't going to expect him to try to fit in right where he left; that would be impossible. I made it a point to let him know he was accepted and loved for the person he was now as much as who he was when he left. It doesn't mean I agreed with all his actions or choices, but I tried not to judge him. He's still my son regardless of changes in his demeanor or personality. With God's help, I wanted to do everything possible to get to know the man who returned, because that man was still my child.

If you are worried about possible changes in your child, or have already seen those changes, what step can you take to show your unconditional love regardless of your feelings about the changes?

What are some specific ways you can ask God to help you to change in order for you to be a less judgmental and more accepting person?

Pray

Lord, I know change is inevitable and all change isn't bad, but I am concerned about how I will handle the changes that may be so evident in my child. Help me to see him through Your eyes, to accept him as You do, and love him with Your love. Thank You. In Jesus' Name, Amen.

by Kathy Guzzo

ACCEPTING *Grace*... AGAIN

The grace of our Lord was poured out on me abundantly, along with the faith and love that are in Christ Jesus.
1 TIMOTHY 1:14

★ ★ ★

WHEN OUR SON TOLD ME of his upcoming second deployment, I didn't listen. After all, his fiancée and I were, at the time, at his base welcoming home his unit from their first deployment to Afghanistan, and he was telling me they would be leaving for Iraq in seven months. My only reaction was to shut out the comment to deal with later, and relish the fact that right now he was back and safe from harm.

As the months passed and he relayed to me all the intense desert training he was doing, I had to face the facts. In a few short months, he would be deploying to Iraq. I learned quickly not to mention his upcoming departure to those not part of the military family. I heard responses like, "Well, this one won't be as bad because you've been through it before," or "God protected him the last time so he'll be fine again," or even, "You're probably so used to him being gone, you won't even miss him." These responses couldn't have been further from the truth. I was dreading this deployment more than the first one because I knew what lay ahead. I knew there'd be sleepless nights when all I could do was pray, that my cell phone would be under my pillow so I wouldn't miss a call, that my heart would skip a beat when the doorbell rang, and that I'd shed tears of grief and relief each time I heard of a casualty. It wasn't an experience I desired to repeat.

However, obviously God was allowing it to happen, so I had to prepare myself. I thought about Mary, and her emotions during Jesus' three years of ministry. When Jesus visited home after being gone for months she must've dreaded knowing He'd leave again, and not knowing when or if she'd see Him again. I can't imagine it ever got easier for her with the animosity toward Him. She must've wanted to keep Him near where she knew what was happening, but she couldn't. As a mom, I'm sure the only way Mary was able to get through the days of Jesus' being gone was the same way I was going to get through—by daily accepting the grace offered by our heavenly Father.

I often quoted to myself, "God will not take me where His grace cannot keep me." God had an abundance of grace to give, and I knew that whatever the next deployment entailed I would need grace for each moment, so I chose to accept all He offered.

Ask

If you're facing a second or even third deployment, how are you better preparing yourself to handle it emotionally? When have you previously felt God's grace in your life and can you honestly say you know His grace is sufficient for you?

Pray

Heavenly Father, I thank You that Your grace is sufficient for me. I pray You will help me accept Your grace daily in order to walk the journey of each day. Thank You for Your abundance of grace, which You offer to me freely and lovingly. In Jesus' Name, Amen.

by Dr. LuAnn Callaway

WE ARE AT *War*

For the sinful nature desires what is contrary to the Spirit, and the Spirit what is contrary to the sinful nature. They are in conflict with each other, so that you do not do what you want.
GALATIANS 5:17

OUR SONS AND DAUGHTERS are bringing down strongholds, where evil has triumphed, in countries around the world. According to Wikipedia we have approximately three million active and reserve United States military personnel. We are actively engaged in two wars and several military actions.

What about those of us who declare our salvation is through Jesus Christ's sacrifice on the cross? Aren't we in a battle too?

A friend of mine carries a nail around in her purse. She says, "It's a reminder that the old fleshly nature is supposed to be dead and in a coffin, but sometimes it raises its ugly head and I have to nail the coffin shut again."

Many Christians who war with the flesh do so because they don't know where the strongholds are located, or they don't want to give them up. A sergeant major recently showed me that before a war can be won, a battalion needs to have certain questions answered.

- How is the stronghold supplied?
- How large is the force within its walls?
- Where does it get its water from?

- How high and thick are its walls?
- What kind of weapons do they have?
- Are enemy reinforcements nearby?

If we fail to allow the Holy Spirit to identify old strongholds (flesh that is still alive and well), we will always be weak in those areas. We are encouraged, however, that it is the job of the Holy Spirit to bring down the strongholds.

The apostle Paul identified the fruit of the flesh (see Galatians 5:19–21), but I am sure it wasn't an exhaustive list. In 2 Corinthians 12:20–21, quarreling, slander, gossip, arrogance, and disorder were added.

Perhaps the Holy Spirit has identified other strongholds that are making you weak in your war.

Ask

My Battle Plan

1. My stronghold______________________________
2. How is this stronghold supplied?____________________
3. Are there people in my life who help supply this stronghold?______________________________
4. Am I serious about the pulling down of this stronghold?
   ____
5. Am I willing to make myself accountable to other Christian sisters?___________________________________

Pray

Dear heavenly Father, may the war of the flesh and the spirit come to an end in my life. I want to be like You more and more each day. I cannot win this war without Your Holy Spirit, who is the One who has all the nails necessary to close the coffin on my flesh as many times as necessary. In Jesus' Name, Amen.

KNOWING JESUS *Personally*

If you have not yet trusted Christ as your Savior, let today be the day that you invite Him to be Lord of your life. Without Christ, we have no hope in this life and no hope of being in heaven in the next. But because of Christ, we can accept eternal life as a free gift based on God's grace!

> "For the wages of sin is death, but the free gift of God is eternal life in Christ Jesus our Lord" (Romans 6:23).

Heaven is not something that we can earn or deserve on our own merits. We can't go to church enough, give enough money to charity, or be good enough in any way to pave our own way to heaven. But the good news is that we don't have to—because God's grace is offered to us as a gift!

> "For by grace you have been saved through faith; and that not of yourselves, it is the gift of God; not as a result of works, so that no one may boast." (Ephesians 2:8–9)

No one deserves to go to heaven, because we sin. Even the best of us do things that displease God.

> "For all have sinned and fall short of the glory of God." (Romans 3:23)

> "There is none who does good, there is not even one." (Romans 3:12)

> "For whoever keeps the whole law and yet stumbles at just one point is guilty of breaking all of it." (James 2:10)

Because God is holy and just, this sin prevents us from being able to be in His presence.

> "The wages of sin is death." (Romans 6:23)

Because God also is not willing that any should perish, He sent His Son Jesus Christ into the world as a perfect, blameless One to die for us. When He did, he paid the penalty for our sins and purchased a place in heaven for us.

> "But God demonstrates his own love toward us: While we

were still sinners, Christ died for us." (Romans 5:8)

"For Christ died for sins once for all, the righteous for the unrighteous, to bring you to God." (1 Peter 3:18)

"Jesus answered, 'I am the way and the truth and the life. No one comes to the Father except through Me.'" (John 14:6)

If you believe this much is true, you're on the right track. But you must go one step further and receive the gift of salvation by placing your personal faith in Christ, asking Him to be your Savior and Lord. Faith is turning from your sins and trusting in Jesus Christ alone for your eternal salvation.

"To all who received Him, to those who believed in his name, he gave the right to become children of God." (John 1:12)

"Everyone who calls on the name of the Lord will be saved." (Romans 10:13)

Are you ready to invite Christ into your life? Pray to Him right now, acknowledging your sin and accepting the free gift of eternal life. Ask Him to show you how to live in a way that honors Him. The suggested prayer below may express the desire of your heart:

Dear Lord, thank You for the gift of eternal life. I know I am a sinner and that I cannot save myself. I believe Jesus is the Son of God and that He died for my sins and rose again from the dead. I now put my complete trust in Him alone for eternal life. Thank You for saving me. Now, help me through Your Holy Spirit to live a life that honors You. In Jesus' Name, Amen.

If you prayed to receive Christ, rejoice! You just made the most important decision that you will ever make in your life. Find someone to share your news with, and seek out a Bible-teaching church where you can spend time with other Christians and learn the Word of God. Make Bible reading and prayer a daily priority, and allow God to mold you into the person He wants you to be.

STAY *Encouraged*

The end of this book doesn't have to be the end of your daily encouragement! Join the online Faith Deployed community at faithdeployed.com where you will find:

- A bonus collection of free downloadable devotions from the *Faith Deployed . . . Again* writers
- Small group study guides for use with both *Faith Deployed* and *Faith Deployed . . . Again*
- An up-to-date list of resources for military families
- A bookstore filled with my favorite titles for military spouses
- An active blog where you'll see more writing from many of this book's contributors
- A list of Christian military wife speakers to consider for your next event
- And more!

Also stay in touch through facebook.com/faithdeployed or twitter.com/faithdeployed for daily uplifting Scriptures, prayer support, and edifying online discussion.

Notes

Section One: Basic Training

1. Joanna Weaver, *Having a Mary Heart in a Martha World* (Colorado Springs: WaterBrook Press, 2007), 38.
2. Jennifer Rothschild, *Self Talk, Soul Talk: What to Say When You Talk to Yourself* (Eugene: Harvest House Publishers, 2007), 48–49.
3. Kathleen Norris, *The Cloister Walk* (New York: Riverhead Books, 1996), 134, 282.
4. Carolyn Custis James, *When Life and Beliefs Collide* (Grand Rapids: Zondervan, 2001), 79.

Section Two: Intimate Allies

1. Sara Horn, *Tour of Duty: Preparing Our Hearts for Deployment* (Nashville: Lifeway Press, 2010), 117.
2. C. S. Lewis, *The Great Divorce* (New York: Macmillan, 1946), 111.
3. For a more in-depth look at what submission and headship look like in the military marriage, see my series of articles called "The Chain of Command in Marriage" at focusonthefamily.com/marriage/military_marriage/the-chain-of-command-in-marriage.aspx.
4. Nancy Leigh DeMoss, *Lies Women Believe: And the Truth That Sets Them Free* (Chicago: Moody, 2001), 143.
5. Gary Thomas, *Sacred Marriage* (Grand Rapids: Zondervan, 2000), 13.
6. Ibid.

Section Three: Tour of Duty

1. Nancie Carmichael, *Surviving One Bad Year* (New York: Simon & Schuster, 2009), 52. Quoting Jonathan Swift from *Jonathan*

Swift: Major Works (Oxford: Oxford University Press, 2008).
2. Carolyn Custis James, *Lost Women of the Bible* (Grand Rapids: Zondervan, 2005), 94.
3. Sara Horn, *Tour of Duty: Preparing Our Hearts for Deployment* (Nashville: LifeWay, 2010), 45.
4. Joyce Meyer, *Battlefield of the Mind Devotional* (New York: Hachette Book Group USA, 2005), 110.
5. Barbara Minar, *Close Connections* (Wheaton: Victor Books, 1992), 188–89.

Section Four: Soul Armor

1. Priscilla Shirer, *Discerning the Voice of God* (Chicago: Moody, 2007), 184.
2. Katherine Morris, "Dealing with Insecurity," wivesinbloom.com/2010/10/dealing-with-insecurity.
3. Cindi McMenamin, *When Women Walk Alone* (Eugene: Harvest House Publishers, 2002), 31–32.
4. Joyce Meyer, *Battlefield of the Mind Devotional* (New York: Hachette Book Group USA, 2005), 212.
5. Alane's book *Notes from the Margins: Healing Conversations with God* chronicles the excruciating losses of her eight babies and journey out of the darkness. It is quite possibly the most God-honoring, life-giving book I have ever read.

Section Five: Stationed in Christ

1. Marshéle Carter Waddell, *Hope for the Home Front* (Virginia Beach: One Hope Ministry, 2003), 131.
2. Sue Monk Kidd, *When the Heart Waits* (New York: HarperOne, 1990), ix.
3. Nancy Leigh DeMoss, *A Place of Quiet Rest* (Chicago: Moody, 2000), 40–41.

Section Six: In God's Service

1. J. W. Follette, *Broken Bread* (Springfield: Gospel Publishing House, 1957), 33. Thanks to Nancie Carmichael for introducing me to Follette on page 54 of her book *Surviving One Bad Year: 7 Spiritual Strategies to Lead You to a New Beginning*.
2. Major Koeman's wife, Benita, founded an invaluable online collection of resources for both military families and for those who want to support them: operationwearehere.com. I have often relied on Benita's vast network and knowledge in my own searches for just the right information for someone.

Section Seven: Home Front Hope

1. Carolyn Custis James, *Lost Women of the Bible* (Grand Rapids: Zondervan, 2005), 134.
2. The program Tonya's husband participated in was the Dave Ramsey Financial Peace University. For more information, see daveramsey.com/fpu. There is also a military-specific version of the program: daveramsey.com/militarycrc/home. The Nashes also recommend the following biblically based books on managing money: *The Total Money Makeover: A Proven Plan for Financial Fitness* by Dave Ramsey; *Financial Peace Revisited* by Dave Ramsey; *Debt-Free Living: Eliminating Debt in a New Economy* by Larry Burkett; and *The Word on Finances: Topical Scriptures and Commentary* by Larry Burkett.
3. If you are interested in hearing more of Nicole's story, visit her blog at marinewifeunplugged.blogspot.com.

Section Eight: For Blue Star Moms

1. Joan Arnold, "Always There," *Hope: Promises to Encourage the Heart* (Minneapolis: Pocket Inspirations, Summerdale Press, 2010).
2. Carolyn Custis James, *Lost Women of the Bible* (Grand Rapids: Zondervan, 2005), 127.

3. Carol Vandesteeg, *When Duty Calls* (Enumclaw: WinePress Publishing, 2001), 160.

Acknowledgments

This book would not have come together if it were not for the efforts of dozens of people.

First, thank you to my husband, Rob, for believing this project was worth two months of frozen dinners and eight weekends (and many evenings) of taking the kids on "field trips" so I could have uninterrupted writing and editing time. There is no way I could have done this without your very practical support!

I'm so grateful for the team of writers who came alongside me for this book. Each one has her own unique ministry to military families and is invaluable: Pam Anderson, Sarah Ball, Rebekah Benimoff, Jill Bozeman, Angela Caban, Dr. LuAnn Callaway, April Lakata Cao, Sharon Carrns, Jessica Culley, Bettina Dowell, Kathleen Edick, Catherine Fitzgerald, Kathy Guzzo, Jill Hart, Patti Katter, Gloria Kroeze, Rachel Latham, Sherry Lightner, Linda Montgomery, Donna Mull, Tonya Nash, Alane Pearce, Pattie Reitz, Claire Shackelford, Sheryl Shearer, Ronda Sturgill, Leeana Tankersley, Marshéle Carter Waddell, and Rosie Williams.

Special thanks to Sherry Lightner for managing the Faith Deployed Facebook ministry (facebook.com/faithdeployed) virtually single-handedly throughout the writing of this book.

Thank you to my agents David Sanford and Tim Beals of Credo Communications, and to Deborah Keiser, Holly Kisly, Pam Pugh, Roslyn Jordan, Janis Backing, and the rest of the team at Moody Publishers for championing the cause of military wives through the publication and promotion of this book.

Above all, I thank my heavenly Father for allowing me to be a small part of what He is already doing to minister to military wives. I am so ordinary, but God is extraordinary. All praise belongs to Him for any healing, comfort, encouragement, or conviction this book may prompt.

MEET THE *Contributors*

Pam Anderson, US Navy

Pam, a Navy wife since 2002, enjoys military life hand-in-hand with husband, Chaplain John Anderson, and daughter, Tiffany. Her undergraduate degree is in sacred music from North Central University, Minneapolis, Minnesota. Pam currently homeschools Tiffany and works as a part-time musician, while keeping the home fires burning. The Andersons currently reside in Princeton, New Jersey.

Sarah Ball, US Army

Sarah grew up on Guam as a missionary kid, then met her husband while attending John Brown University. She taught middle school for several years, then switched to full-time ministry at home. Each new duty station has brought opportunities to meet and minister through Protestant Women of the Chapel, MOPS, Awana, chapel programs, family readiness groups, and neighborhood friendships. She is currently adventuring into homeschooling and enjoying a respite between deployments. Sarah feels blessed to minister with her Army chaplain husband, Doug, and children: Rachel, Robert, Laura, and Levi.

Rebekah Benimoff, US Army

Rebekah and her husband, Roger, live in Dallas with their two sons. Roger is a retired Army chaplain whose memoir *Faith Under Fire* (Crown 2009) focuses on how his time in Iraq challenged his faith and marriage as he struggled with PTSD and Compassion Fatigue upon his return home. Rebekah contributed the "spouse and family perspective" to their book. (Read more about her journey at redbookmag.com/health-wellness/ptsd-after-iraq.) Rebekah works for the Coalition to Salute America's Heroes, and blogs at ladiesbydesign.com and faithdeployed.com.

Jill S. Bozeman, US Army

Jill is a sixteen-year veteran spouse of SSG Wade C. Bozeman. Jill is the mother of two creative and heroic children, as well as the founder and national director of a pro-marriage program for spouses of deployed service members called *Operation Faithful Support*. The Bozeman family is currently serving our country and our Lord Jesus Christ at Fort Knox, Kentucky, and attends Heritage International Christian Church in Radcliff.

Angela Caban, US Army National Guard

Angela Caban is a freelance writer and military columnist. Her husband, Vincent, has been in the Army for more than thirteen years and was deployed in 2008; he was one of the many soldiers impacted by the unprecedented activation of the National Guard. In 2010, Angela launched the Homefront United Network (homefrontunited.com), a military spouse and family support website offering support through positive encouragement. She is a key volunteer for the National Military Family Association and Operation Homefront. She and Vincent have one son, and currently reside in Pennsylvania. For more on Angela visit angelacaban.com or e-mail her at angela@angelacaban.com.

Dr. LuAnn Callaway, Blue Star Mom

LuAnn has been a Christian counselor for thirty-one years and in private practice for fifteen of those years. She is the National Counseling Director of Military Ministry, a division of Campus Crusade for Christ. She is a speaker for Focus on the Family, American Association of Christian Counselors, military chaplain conferences, and Warrior Transition Battalions. She and her husband, Sid, live in Stockbridge, Georgia. Their son, Jacob, returned from a tour in Afghanistan with the 48th Infantry, Georgia National Guard in March 2010.

April Lakata Cao, US Navy
April lives in Virginia Beach, Virginia. April and her husband, an Explosive Ordnance Disposal Officer and graduate of the United States Naval Academy, have two beautiful children. As a military spouse who has endured five deployments and eight moves, April shares her challenges and life lessons as a published writer and regular contributor to faithdeployed.com and wivesinbloom.com. Her blog, Amazing Grace (intoourheart.blogspot.com), encourages, educates, and inspires adoptive and prospective adoptive families. April considers being a stay-at-home mom her most important work.

Sharon Carrns, US Army and Blue Star Mom
As an Army wife, Sharon volunteered with Army Community Service, was inducted into the Order of Saint Joan of Arc and received the Helping Hands Award from the III Corps Commanding General of the US Army for helping Army families adjust to Army life. Her daughter served in the Army for four years, and her son-in-law still serves. Sharon Carrns has also authored workbooks to accompany fiction and nonfiction books, church ministry, and corporate studies. She lives in Spring Lake, Michigan, with her husband, daughter, and son.

Jessica Culley, US Coast Guard
Jessica Culley grew up in Montana and graduated from the Coast Guard Academy in 1998. Following graduation, she served aboard a Medium Endurance Cutter and spent some time at a Marine Safety Detachment. She and her husband, John, were married in 1999. John continues to serve on active duty with the Coast Guard. Jessica currently homeschools their two children, Dominic and Marissa. She is also actively involved in PWOC (Protestant Women of the Chapel) with leadership on both the local and regional levels.

Bettina Dowell, US Navy Reserves

As a military wife for more than twenty-nine years, Bettina treasures the opportunity to serve military spouses. In 2010 she and her husband, Rob, celebrated both his homecoming from Iraq and his retirement from the Navy. They have two sons and a daughter-in-law pursuing artistic careers in Los Angeles and a high school daughter (Libby—Bettina's cowriter on "Gimmes for Teens") at home with them outside Washington, D.C. Bettina is a speaker, and a contributing blogger at faithdeployed.com and wivesoffaith.org and enjoys writing on her own blog at simplestoriestimelesstruths.blogspot.com.

Kathleen Edick, Blue Star Mom

Kathleen Edick and her husband, Don, of northern Colorado, are proud parents of four children and two grandchildren. Having come from a long line of those who have given service to our nation, Kathleen says her heart for the military family comes naturally. Drawing on her love of children and family, art and truth-telling, she along with her friend and business partner Paula J. Johnson write and illustrate the warm and touching children's book series *We Serve Too!* bringing "Honor and Courage for Military Kids." All *We Serve Too!* books and resources can be found at weservetoo.com.

Catherine Fitzgerald, US Marine Corps

Catherine is married to a Marine helicopter pilot stationed in Jacksonville, North Carolina. Together they have a daughter, Grace. Catherine graduated from North Carolina State University with a BA in psychology and earned her K–6 teaching certification from Meredith College. She leads a ministry for military families at her home church and has written a group study guide for *Faith Deployed* (see faithdeployed.com) as well as various articles for the site. Her work has also been published in *Proverbs 31 Magazine* and other websites.

Kathy Guzzo, Blue Star Mom

Kathy Guzzo is the mother of four adult children and the author of several articles for military families, including the brochure *Deployment, What's A Family To Do?* Her son served in the USMC from 2004–08, and was deployed to both Iraq and Afghanistan. She is the coordinator for Hope at Home Ministry in Rockford, Illinois, serving women with loved ones in the military. She also writes a biweekly newsletter sharing encouragement and resources with women across the country. Kathy and her husband, Mickey, live in Rockford, Illinois.

Jill Hart, US Air Force

Jill Hart is the founder of Christian Work at Home Moms (CWAHM.com) and coauthor of *So You Want To Be a Work-at-Home Mom*. Jill and her husband, Allen, reside in Nebraska with their two children. During Allen's military career, he and Jill served as leaders in the Protestant Youth of the Chapel (PYOC) program and worked closely with the Navigator and Cadence ministries on base. Allen now works as a computer contractor on the base where he served. They enjoy being a part of the military community they live in, serving those who are serving our country.

Patti Katter, US Army

Patti Gallion Katter is the wife of a combat disabled veteran who served in the US Marine Corps and in the US Army. Patti is the mother of three beautiful children. In April of 2007, Patti created a terrific interactive website called Christian Military Wives. Christian Military Wives is now a 501c3 nonprofit ministry of Christian Military Fellowship. If you are looking to fellowship with other military wives, be sure to check out CMWives.org.

Gloria Kroeze, Blue Star Mom

Gloria D. Kroeze and her husband, Nick, live in Grand Rapids, Michigan. They have two daughters and two sons. One of their sons is a Marine and one of their sons-in-law is an Army chaplain. Five grandchildren brighten up their lives. Gloria is a chaplain at Helen DeVos Children's Hospital.

Rachel Latham, US Army National Guard

Rachel Latham makes her home in Bon Aqua, Tennessee, with her husband, Ken, four children, and assorted pets. She is a homemaker and writer and enjoys gardening and martial arts in her spare time. Rachel's husband has served twenty years in the Army and is on his third deployment overseas. He is currently with the Tennessee Army National Guard. Rachel and Ken have been married for seventeen years and are members of Bethel Baptist Church in Dickson, Tennessee. Rachel has written for *Foundations*, FaithDeployed.com, WivesofFaith.org, and *Hearts at Home* magazines. Follow her blog, Scattered Words, at rachellatham.blogspot.com.

Sherry Lightner, US Army National Guard

Sherry Lightner currently lives in Ballston Lake, New York, with her husband of twenty years and their four children. Her husband is a Signal Warrant Officer for the Army National Guard. Sherry serves as a homemaker and enjoys leading and participating in small group Bible studies, and children's ministries such as AWANA. Sherry is a regular columnist for faithdeployed.com and serves as an administrator for the Faith Deployed Facebook page.

Linda Montgomery, US Air Force and Blue Star Mom

Linda Montgomery serves with her husband, Mike, in Hampton Roads, Virginia, as full-time field missionaries with Military Ministry of Campus Crusade for Christ. They are the coauthors of the FamilyLife Bible study *Making Your Marriage*

Deployment Ready. Linda is the founder, managing editor, and a contributing writer for Military Ministry's online devotional Excellent or Praiseworthy (excellentorpraiseworthy.org). Their twenty-three years of active duty service took them around the world as an Air Force family until Mike's retirement as a colonel in 1995. They are the parents of two grown children and will be happy to tell you about their grandchildren.

Donna Mull, Blue Star Mom
Donna Mull is the mother of Army National Guard Captain Jason Mull who served in Iraq in 2008. She lives in a picturesque Rhode Island town that hosts the nation's oldest, longstanding Fourth of July parade honoring civil and military servants (225 successive years). Donna is the author of *A Prayer Journey through Deployment*, a collection of military prayer devotionals highlighting specific needs of soldiers and their families.

Tonya Nash, US Air Force
Tonya Nash is in her eighth year of on-the-job training as a military wife. She and her husband, Jamie, have been through three deployments and three military moves. They have one son. Tonya has a master's degree in public health and is a graduate of the Jerry B. Jenkins Christian Writers Guild Apprentice Program. She is a frequent contributor to *Military Spouse Magazine* and several online websites. She and Jamie are passionate about helping people get out of debt and have served on the financial counseling team at their church. For more about Tonya, visit christianmommywriter.com.

Alane Pearce, US Air Force
Alane Pearce is a military spouse with a heart to help women see light in the darkness of life's trials. She is the author of *Notes from the Margins: Healing Conversations with God* and its companion Bible study, *Comparing Notes*. Alane is also the founder and executive director of Wings for Women Military

Spouse Conferences to offer hope and encouragement to military spouses worldwide. She lives wherever the Air Force sends them.

Pattie Reitz, US Air Force

Pattie Reitz is the proud wife of her Air Force chaplain husband, Roland, and this year they celebrate twenty years of marriage and ministry together, nine with the military. They have two daughters, Mackenzie and Meredith. Pattie holds a BA from Southwest Baptist University and her MS Ed from Northwest Missouri State University, both in English education. She taught high school and college English for more than ten years before her husband joined active duty service in 2006. Pattie has served with the chapel praise team, OSC, PWOC, and with WivesofFaith.org as a writer and editor.

Claire Shackelford, US Army and Blue Star Mom

Claire earned her master's in social work with a concentration in community and nonprofit organizing from the University of South Carolina, Columbia. Her husband, Bryan, served in the Army until an accident in training left him unable to continue in his service. Bryan and Claire have four children, one of whom is active Army and has deployed twice, and one of whom is in the reserves. Claire works as a ministry leader with Christian Military Wives, and serves on the board of directors for Christian Military Fellowship. Claire also writes for various military blogs and is a regular contributor at *Wives in Bloom*, the online magazine for Christian Military Wives.

Sheryl Shearer, US Navy

Sheryl is a teacher, author, and the spouse of an active-duty Navy chaplain. She is mom and home educator to their four daughters, and a teacher at Homeschool Plus in Norfolk, Virginia. Her degrees are in music (BA, MSU-Moorhead) and theology (MATS, MDiv, Assemblies of God Theological

Seminary). During seventeen years of married life, Sheryl and Brian have weathered thirteen moves. Sheryl enjoys reading, blogging, writing, discussing politics, playing the piano, running, traveling, playing the Scrabble app, and watching Duke basketball and Steeler football games. Her favorite tours were in Germany and Kaneohe Bay, Hawaii.

Ronda Sturgill, US Air Force
The wife of an Air Force chaplain, Ronda is the author of three Bible studies: *Wives of the Warriors, Living Confidently in Christ,* available at pleasantword.com; *Desperate Housecries: Discovering Genuine Hope in God;* and *Extreme Makeover: Heart Edition.* With a passion for teaching God's Word, she often speaks at women's retreats and conferences and would love to speak at yours! She and her husband are currently stationed at Dover AFB in Delaware. To contact Ronda, visit her at rondasturgill.com.

Leeana Tankersley, US Navy
Born and raised in San Diego, Leeana holds English degrees from Liberty University and West Virginia University. In 2003, Leeana married Steve, an active duty Navy SEAL. They spent their first year of marriage stationed in Bahrain, an experience she recorded in her first book: *Found Art: Discovering Beauty in Foreign Places* (Zondervan 2009). In addition to writing and speaking, Leeana offers Found Art workshops and retreats that create space for self-reflection and self-expression. In 2008, Leeana and Steve welcomed boy/girl twins, Luke Stephen and Lane Watkins. Follow Leeana at GypsyInk.com.

Marshéle Carter Waddell, US Navy and Blue Star Mom
Marshéle Carter Waddell served with her husband, CDR (ret) Mark Waddell, a career US Navy SEAL, for twenty-five years around the world. Today, her husband is a disabled combat veteran with PTSD and multiple TBIs, and her son is an active duty Marine. She is the author of *Hope for the Home Front:*

Winning the Emotional and Spiritual Battles of a Military Wife and its companion Bible study, and coauthor of *When War Comes Home: Christ-centered Healing for Wives of Combat Veterans.* For information on When War Comes Home retreats, visit: whenwarcomeshomeretreats.com.

Rosie Williams, US Army

Rosie's husband, Steve, is a Vietnam veteran who was an Army infantryman (Point Man) with the 101st Airborne Division. Steve and Rosie work with Point Man, a Christian organization for vets, led by vets. Rosie has a BS degree in family and child development from Kansas State. Rosie has provided leadership and planning for four national Home Front Retreats and helps to set up Home Front Groups across Kansas to meet the needs of wives (or moms or daughters) of veterans or active military families. She is a public speaker and freelance writer and lives in Topeka, Kansas.

ABOUT THE *Author*

Jocelyn Green, the wife of a former Coast Guard officer, is an award-winning author, freelance writer, and editor. She is the author of *Faith Deployed: Daily Encouragement for Military Wives* (Moody 2008), along with fourteen contributing writers. She is also coauthor of *Battlefields & Blessings: Stories of Faith and Courage from the War in Iraq/Afghanistan* (AMG Publishers, 2009). Her books won the Bronze and Gold Medals, respectively, from the Military Writers Society of America (religious/spiritual category) in 2010. Her website for military wives, faithdeployed.com, won third place in a national contest held by the Evangelical Press Association in 2010.

She is the editor for WivesinBloom.com, the online magazine of Christian Military Wives (a branch of Christian Military Fellowship) and a contributor to the website StartMarriageRight.com. Jocelyn's Facebook page for military wives (facebook.com/faithdeployed) has the largest following of any other Christian military wife page on Facebook to date.

Jocelyn graduated from Taylor University in Upland, Indiana, with a BA in English, concentration in writing. She is a frequent speaker at military wife events, women's church groups, and writers conferences, and is an active member of the Evangelical Press Association, Christian Authors Network, the Advanced Writers and Speakers Association, and the Military Writers Society of America.

Jocelyn and her husband, Rob, have two children and live in Cedar Falls, Iowa. Visit her at jocelyngreen.com or drop her a line at jocelyn@jocelyngreen.com.